APPETIZERS

Microwave Cooking: Microwave ovens vary in wattage. Use the cooking times as guidelines and check for doneness before adding more time.

Preparation/Cooking Times: Preparation times are based on the approximate amount of time required to assemble the recipe before cooking, baking, chilling or serving. These times include preparation steps such as measuring, chopping and mixing. The fact that some preparations and cooking can be done simultaneously is taken into account. Preparation of optional ingredients and serving suggestions is not included.

TABLE OF CONTENTS

Pizza Fondue, page 30

Celebration Cheese Ball, page 44

Maple-Glazed Meatballs, page 46

FAMOUS CLASSICS

Original Ranch® Snack Mix

8 cups KELLOGG'S® CRISPIX® cereal
2½ cups small pretzels
2½ cups bite-size Cheddar cheese crackers (optional)
3 tablespoons vegetable oil
1 packet (1 ounce) HIDDEN VALLEY® The Original Ranch®
Salad Dressing & Seasoning Mix

Combine cereal, pretzels and crackers in a gallon-size Glad® Zipper Storage Bag. Pour oil over mixture. Seal bag and toss to coat. Add salad dressing & seasoning mix; seal bag and toss again until coated.

Makes 10 cups mix

Original Ranch® Oyster Crackers

1 box (16 ounces) oyster crackers
¼ cup vegetable oil
1 packet (1 ounce) HIDDEN VALLEY® The Original Ranch®
Salad Dressing & Seasoning Mix

Place crackers in a gallon size Glad® Fresh Protection Bag. Pour oil over crackers and toss to coat. Add salad dressing & seasoning mix; toss again until coated. Bake at 250°F for 15 to 20 minutes.

Makes 8 cups crackers

Top to bottom: Original Ranch® Snack Mix and Original Ranch® Oyster Crackers

Hot Artichoke Dip

1 envelope LIPTON® RECIPE SECRETS® Onion Soup Mix*
1 can (14 ounces) artichoke hearts, drained and chopped
1 cup HELLMANN'S® or BEST FOODS® Mayonnaise
1 container (8 ounces) sour cream
1 cup shredded Swiss or mozzarella cheese (about 4 ounces)

*Also terrific with LIPTON® RECIPE SECRETS® Savory Herb with Garlic, Golden Onion or Onion-Mushroom Soup Mix.

1. Preheat oven to 350°F. In 1-quart casserole, combine all ingredients.

2. Bake, uncovered, 30 minutes or until heated through.

3. Serve with your favorite dippers.   *Makes 3 cups dip*

Cold Artichoke Dip: Omit Swiss cheese. Stir in, if desired, ¼ cup grated Parmesan cheese. Do not bake.

Serving Suggestion: When serving hot dip for a party, try baking it in 2 smaller casseroles. When the first casserole is empty, replace it with the second one, fresh from the oven.

Zesty Liver Pâté

⅓ cup butter or margarine
 1 pound chicken livers
¾ cup coarsely chopped green onions
¾ cup chopped fresh parsley
½ cup dry white wine
¾ teaspoon TABASCO® brand Pepper Sauce
½ teaspoon salt
    Crackers or French bread

Melt butter in large saucepan; add chicken livers, onions and parsley. Sauté until livers are evenly browned and cooked through. Transfer to blender or food processor container. Add wine, TABASCO® Sauce and salt; cover. Process until smooth. Pour into decorative crock-style jar with lid. Chill until thick enough to spread. Serve with crackers or French bread.

Makes about 2 cups pâté

Hot Artichoke Dip

Spicy Shrimp Cocktail

2 tablespoons olive or vegetable oil
¼ cup finely chopped onion
1 tablespoon chopped green bell pepper
1 clove garlic, minced
1 can (8 ounces) CONTADINA® Tomato Sauce
1 tablespoon chopped pitted green olives, drained
¼ teaspoon red pepper flakes
1 pound cooked shrimp, chilled

1. Heat oil in small skillet. Add onion, bell pepper and garlic; sauté until vegetables are tender. Stir in tomato sauce, olives and red pepper flakes.

2. Bring to a boil; simmer, uncovered, for 5 minutes. Cover.

3. Chill thoroughly. Combine sauce with shrimp in small bowl.

Makes 8 servings

Prep Time: 6 minutes
Cook Time: 10 minutes

Ortega® 7-Layer Dip

1 can (16 ounces) ORTEGA® Refried Beans
1 package (1.25 ounces) ORTEGA® Taco Seasoning Mix
1 container (8 ounces) sour cream
1 container (8 ounces) refrigerated guacamole
1 cup (4 ounces) shredded Cheddar cheese
1 cup ORTEGA® Salsa Prima Homestyle Mild or Thick & Chunky
1 can (4 ounces) ORTEGA® Diced Green Chiles
2 large green onions, sliced
   Tortilla chips

COMBINE beans and seasoning mix in small bowl. Spread bean mixture in 8-inch square baking dish.

TOP with sour cream, guacamole, cheese, salsa, chiles and green onions. Serve with chips.

Makes 10 to 12 servings

Note: Can be prepared up to 2 hours ahead and refrigerated.

Spicy Shrimp Cocktail

Artichoke Frittata

1 can (14 ounces) artichoke hearts, drained
1 tablespoon olive oil, divided
½ cup minced green onions
5 eggs
½ cup (2 ounces) shredded Swiss cheese
2 tablespoons grated Parmesan cheese
1 tablespoon minced fresh parsley
1 teaspoon salt
Freshly ground black pepper to taste

1. Chop artichoke hearts; set aside.

2. Heat 2 teaspoons oil in 10-inch skillet over medium heat. Add green onions; cook and stir until tender. Remove from skillet.

3. Beat eggs in medium bowl until light. Stir in artichokes, green onions, cheeses, parsley, salt and pepper.

4. Heat remaining 1 teaspoon oil in same skillet over medium heat. Pour egg mixture into skillet. Cook 4 to 5 minutes or until bottom is lightly browned. Place large plate over skillet and invert frittata onto plate. Return frittata, uncooked side down, to skillet. Cook about 4 minutes more or until center is just set. Cut into small wedges.   *Makes 12 to 16 appetizer servings*

Lipton® Onion Dip

1 envelope LIPTON® RECIPE SECRETS® Onion Soup Mix
1 container (16 ounces) sour cream

1. In medium bowl, combine ingredients; chill, if desired.

2. Serve with your favorite dippers.   *Makes 2 cups dip*

Salsa Onion Dip: Stir in ½ cup of your favorite salsa.

Prep Time: 5 minutes

Artichoke Frittata

Spinach Dip

1 package (10 ounces) frozen chopped spinach, thawed and squeezed dry
1 container (16 ounces) sour cream
1 cup HELLMANN'S® or BEST FOODS® Mayonnaise
1 package KNORR® Recipe Classics™ Vegetable Soup, Dip and Recipe Mix
1 can (8 ounces) water chestnuts, drained and chopped (optional)
3 green onions, chopped

● In medium bowl, combine all ingredients; chill at least 2 hours to blend flavors.

● Stir before serving. Serve with your favorite dippers.

Makes about 4 cups dip

Yogurt Spinach Dip: Substitute 1 container (16 ounces) plain lowfat yogurt for sour cream.

Spinach and Cheese Dip: Add 2 cups (8 ounces) shredded Swiss cheese with spinach.

Prep Time: 10 minutes
Chill Time: 2 hours

Spicy Cheese 'n' Chili Dip

1 pound BOB EVANS® Special Seasonings Roll Sausage
1 pound pasteurized process cheese spread
1 (10-ounce) can diced tomatoes with green chiles, drained
1 (14- to 16-ounce) bag tortilla chips

Crumble and cook sausage in medium skillet until browned. Drain on paper towels. Combine cheese and tomatoes in medium saucepan; heat until cheese is melted. Stir in sausage. Serve in warm bowl with tortilla chips.

Makes 10 to 12 servings

Spinach Dip

Festive Franks

1 can (8 ounces) reduced-fat crescent roll dough
5½ teaspoons barbecue sauce
⅓ cup finely shredded reduced-fat sharp Cheddar cheese
8 fat-free hot dogs
¼ teaspoon poppy seeds (optional)
Additional barbecue sauce (optional)

1. Preheat oven to 350°F. Spray large baking sheet with nonstick cooking spray; set aside.

2. Unroll dough and separate into 8 triangles. Cut each triangle in half lengthwise to make 2 triangles. Lightly spread barbecue sauce over each triangle. Sprinkle with cheese.

3. Cut each hot dog in half; trim off rounded ends. Place one hot dog piece at large end of one dough triangle. Roll up jelly-roll style from wide end. Place point-side down on prepared baking sheet. Sprinkle with poppy seeds, if desired. Repeat with remaining hot dog pieces and dough.

4. Bake 13 minutes or until golden brown. Cool 1 to 2 minutes on baking sheet. Serve with additional barbecue sauce for dipping, if desired.

Makes 16 servings

Buffalo-Style Chicken Nachos

2 cups diced cooked chicken
⅓ cup *Frank's® RedHot® Original Cayenne Pepper Sauce*
2 tablespoons melted butter
1 bag (10 ounces) tortilla chips
3 cups shredded Cheddar or Monterey Jack cheese

1. Preheat oven to 350°F. Combine chicken, *Frank's RedHot* Sauce and butter. Layer chips, chicken and cheese in ovenproof serving dish or baking dish.

2. Bake 5 minutes just until cheese melts. Garnish as desired. Splash on more *Frank's RedHot* Sauce to taste.

Makes 4 to 8 servings

Prep Time: 5 minutes
Cook Time: 5 minutes

Festive Franks

FAST & FABULOUS

Creamy Garlic Salsa Dip

1 envelope LIPTON® RECIPE SECRETS® Savory Herb with Garlic Soup Mix*

1 container (16 ounces) sour cream

½ cup your favorite prepared salsa

*Also terrific with LIPTON® RECIPE SECRETS® Onion Soup Mix.

1. In medium bowl, combine all ingredients; chill at least 2 hours.

2. Serve with your favorite dippers.   *Makes 2½ cups dip*

Alouette® Elégante with Red Pepper Coulis

1 small jar roasted red peppers, drained

1 teaspoon olive oil

1 (6-ounce) package ALOUETTE® Elégante, Roasted Garlic and Pesto

Paprika

Fresh chopped chives or parsley

To make red pepper coulis, add roasted red peppers and olive oil to food processor; purée until smooth. Pour coulis into center of 8-inch rimmed salad plate (a plain white plate works best). Position Alouette Elégante in center of coulis. Sprinkle paprika and chopped chives around rim of plate. Serve with your favorite crusty bread.   *Makes 6 to 8 servings*

Creamy Garlic Salsa Dip

Piggy Wraps

1 package HILLSHIRE FARM® Lit'l Smokies
**2 cans (8 ounces each) refrigerated crescent roll dough,
cut into small triangles**

Preheat oven to 400°F.

Wrap individual Lit'l Smokies in dough triangles. Bake 5 minutes or until
golden brown. *Makes about 50 hors d'oeuvres*

Note: Piggy Wraps may be frozen. To reheat in microwave, microwave at
HIGH (100% power) 1½ minutes or at MEDIUM-HIGH (70% power)
2 minutes. When reheated in microwave, dough will not be crisp.

Lit'l Party Delights

¾ cup chili sauce
¾ cup grape jelly
4 teaspoons red wine
2 teaspoons dry mustard
1½ teaspoons soy sauce
½ teaspoon ground ginger
½ teaspoon ground cinnamon
½ teaspoon ground nutmeg
1 pound HILLSHIRE FARM® Lit'l Smokies

Combine chili sauce, jelly, wine, mustard, soy sauce, ginger, cinnamon and
nutmeg in medium saucepan; heat and stir over medium heat until mixture is
smooth. Add Lit'l Smokies; heat 5 to 6 minutes or until hot. Serve with frilled
toothpicks. *Makes about 50 hors d'oeuvres*

Top to bottom: Piggy Wraps and Lit'l Party Delights

Pizza Snack Cups

- **1 can (12 ounces) refrigerated biscuits (10 biscuits)**
- **½ pound ground beef**
- **1 jar (14 ounces) RAGÚ® Pizza Quick® Sauce**
- **½ cup shredded mozzarella cheese (about 2 ounces)**

Preheat oven to 375°F. In muffin pan, evenly press 1 biscuit on bottom and up side of each cup; chill until ready to fill.

In 10-inch skillet, brown ground beef over medium-high heat; drain. Stir in Ragú Pizza Quick Sauce and heat through.

Evenly spoon beef mixture into prepared muffin cups. Bake 15 minutes. Sprinkle with cheese and bake an additional 5 minutes or until cheese is melted and biscuits are golden. Let stand 5 minutes. Gently remove pizza cups from muffin pan and serve. *Makes 10 pizza cups*

Prep Time: 10 minutes
Cook Time: 25 minutes

Brandied Apricot Brie

- **1 wheel ALOUETTE® Baby Brie™, Plain**
- **1 cup apricot preserves**
- **1 tablespoon freshly squeezed orange juice**
- **2 teaspoons brandy**
- **1 teaspoon ground cinnamon**
- **1 loaf French bread, sliced**

MICROWAVE DIRECTIONS

Combine preserves, orange juice, brandy and cinnamon in microwave-safe bowl. Cover with plastic wrap and microwave on HIGH (100% power) 1½ minutes or until sauce begins to bubble. Place ALOUETTE® Baby Brie™ in shallow dish and top with apricot sauce. Microwave, uncovered, on HIGH 30 to 90 seconds or until cheese softens. Serve with French bread.

Makes 6 to 8 servings

Pizza Snack Cups

Pizza Rollers

1 package (10 ounces) refrigerated pizza dough
½ cup pizza sauce
18 slices turkey pepperoni
6 sticks mozzarella cheese

1. Preheat oven to 425°F. Coat baking sheet with nonstick cooking spray.

2. Roll out pizza dough on baking sheet to form 12×9-inch rectangle. Cut pizza dough into 6 (4½×4-inch) rectangles. Spread about 1 tablespoon sauce over center third of each rectangle. Top with 3 slices pepperoni and stick of mozzarella cheese. Bring ends of dough together over cheese, pinching to seal. Place seam side down on prepared baking sheet.

3. Bake in center of oven 10 minutes or until golden brown.

Makes 6 servings

Chicken Nachos

22 (about 1 ounce) GUILTLESS GOURMET® Baked Tortilla Chips (yellow, red or blue corn)
½ cup (4 ounces) cooked and shredded boneless chicken breast
¼ cup chopped green onions
¼ cup (1 ounce) grated Cheddar cheese
Sliced green and red chilies (optional)

MICROWAVE DIRECTIONS

Spread tortilla chips on flat microwave-safe plate. Sprinkle chicken, onions and cheese over chips. Microwave on HIGH 30 seconds until cheese starts to bubble. Serve hot. Garnish with chilies, if desired.

CONVENTIONAL DIRECTIONS

Preheat oven to 325°F. Spread tortilla chips on baking sheet. Sprinkle chicken, onions and cheese over chips. Bake about 5 minutes or until cheese starts to bubble. Serve hot.

Makes 22 nachos

Pizza Rollers

Herb Cheese Twists

2 tablespoons butter or margarine
¼ cup grated Parmesan cheese
1 teaspoon dried parsley flakes
1 teaspoon dried basil leaves
1 can (7½ ounces) refrigerated buttermilk biscuits

1. Preheat oven to 400°F. Microwave butter in small bowl at MEDIUM (50% power) just until melted; cool slightly. Stir in cheese, parsley and basil. Set aside.

2. Pat each biscuit into 5×2-inch rectangle. Spread 1 teaspoon butter mixture on each rectangle; cut each in half lengthwise. Twist each strip 3 or 4 times. Place on lightly greased baking sheet. Bake 8 to 10 minutes or until golden brown. *Makes 5 servings*

Prep and Cook Time: 20 minutes

Tortilla Roll-Ups

1 (8-ounce) package cream cheese
1 cup chopped black olives
4 green onions, chopped
2 teaspoons TABASCO® brand Pepper Sauce
4 to 6 large flour tortillas

Combine cream cheese, olives, green onions and TABASCO® Sauce in medium bowl. Spread thin layer of cream cheese mixture on each tortilla. Starting at one end, gently roll tortilla into tight tube. Wrap with plastic wrap; chill until ready to serve. To serve, unwrap roll, trim edges of tortilla and slice into 8 (1-inch) slices. Serve slices cut sides up. *Makes 32 to 48 pieces*

Herb Cheese Twists

Quick Pimiento Cheese Snacks

- **2 ounces reduced-fat cream cheese, softened**
- **½ cup (2 ounces) shredded reduced-fat Cheddar cheese**
- **1 jar (2 ounces) diced pimiento, drained**
- **2 tablespoons finely chopped pecans**
- **½ teaspoon hot pepper sauce**
- **24 French bread slices, about ¼ inch thick, or party bread slices**

1. Preheat broiler.

2. Combine cream cheese and Cheddar cheese in small bowl; mix well. Stir in pimiento, pecans and hot pepper sauce.

3. Place bread slices on broiler pan or nonstick baking sheet. Broil, 4 inches from heat, 1 to 2 minutes or until lightly toasted on both sides.

4. Spread cheese mixture evenly onto bread slices. Broil 1 to 2 minutes or until cheese mixture is hot and bubbly. Transfer to serving plate; garnish, if desired. *Makes 24 servings*

Chavrie® Quesadilla

- **½ cup drained cooked black beans**
- **½ cup drained chunky tomato salsa**
- **6 (6-inch) flour tortillas**
- **1 (5.3-ounce) package CHAVRIE®, Plain or Basil & Roasted Garlic**
- **2 teaspoons olive oil**

Combine black beans and salsa; spread onto 3 tortillas.

Lightly toast remaining 3 tortillas in oiled skillet.

Spread Chavrie onto toasted tortillas in skillet; place on top of black bean mixture to make "sandwich."

Add olive oil to skillet. Heat quesadillas in skillet over medium heat until cheese starts to soften and tortilla starts to brown. Cut into wedges.
Makes 6 to 9 servings

Quick Pimiento Cheese Snacks

Summer Sausage Dippers

  5 **ounces sharp Cheddar cheese, cut into 1 × ½-inch chunks**
 32 **pimiento-stuffed green olives**
  1 **(9-ounce) HILLSHIRE FARM® Summer Sausage, cut into**
     32 thick half-moon slices
  1 **cup ketchup**
 ½ **cup apricot jam or preserves**
  1 **tablespoon cider vinegar**
  2 **teaspoons Worcestershire sauce**

Secure 1 piece cheese and 1 olive onto 1 Summer Sausage slice with frilled toothpick; repeat with remaining cheese, olives and sausage. Arrange on platter. Cover and refrigerate until ready to serve. For dipping sauce, stir ketchup, jam, vinegar and Worcestershire sauce in small saucepan; heat over medium-low heat until warm and smooth. Serve sausage dippers with sauce.

Makes 16 servings

Spicy Mustard Kielbasa Bites

  1 **pound whole kielbasa or smoked Polish sausage**
  1 **cup *French's*® Spicy Brown Mustard**
 ¾ **cup honey**
  1 **tablespoon *Frank's*® *RedHot*® Cayenne Pepper Sauce**

1. Place kielbasa on grid. Grill over medium heat 10 minutes or until lightly browned, turning occasionally. Cut into bite-sized pieces; set aside.

2. Combine mustard and honey in large saucepan. Bring to a boil over medium heat. Stir in kielbasa and *Frank's RedHot* Sauce. Cook until heated through. Transfer to serving bowl. Serve with party toothpicks.

Makes 16 servings

Note: Refrigerate leftover honey-mustard mixture. This makes a tasty dip for chicken nuggets, cooked chicken wings or mini hot dogs.

Prep Time: 15 minutes
Cook Time: 10 minutes

Summer Sausage Dippers

DIPS & SPREADS

Pizza Fondue

½ **pound bulk Italian sausage**
1 **cup chopped onion**
2 **jars (26 ounces each) meatless pasta sauce**
4 **ounces thinly sliced ham, finely chopped**
1 **package (3 ounces) sliced pepperoni, finely chopped**
¼ **teaspoon red pepper flakes**
1 **pound mozzarella cheese, cut into ¾-inch cubes**
1 **loaf Italian or French bread, cut into 1-inch cubes**

SLOW COOKER DIRECTIONS

1. Cook sausage and onion in large skillet until sausage is browned. Drain off fat.

2. Transfer sausage mixture to slow cooker. Stir in pasta sauce, ham, pepperoni and pepper flakes. Cover; cook on LOW 3 to 4 hours.

3. Serve fondue with cheese cubes and bread cubes.

Makes 20 to 25 appetizer servings

Prep Time: 15 minutes
Cook Time: 3 to 4 hours

Pizza Fondue

Creamy Artichoke-Parmesan Dip

    2 cans (14 ounces each) quartered artichokes,
        drained and chopped
    2 cups (8 ounces) shredded mozzarella cheese
 1½ cups grated Parmesan cheese
 1½ cups mayonnaise
    ½ cup finely chopped onion
    ½ teaspoon dried oregano leaves
    ¼ teaspoon garlic powder
        Pita wedges
        Assorted cut-up vegetables

SLOW COOKER DIRECTIONS

1. Place all ingredients except pita wedges and vegetables into slow cooker; stir to blend well. Cover; cook on LOW 2 hours.

2. Serve with pita wedges and vegetables.   *Makes 4 cups dip*

Vegetable Hummus

    2 cloves garlic
    2 cans (15 to 19 ounces each) chick peas or garbanzo beans,
        rinsed and drained
    1 package KNORR® Recipe Classics™ Vegetable Soup, Dip and
        Recipe Mix
    ½ cup water
    ½ cup BERTOLLI® Olive Oil
    2 tablespoons lemon juice
    ¼ teaspoon ground cumin
    6 (8-inch) whole wheat or white pita breads, cut into wedges

• In food processor, pulse garlic until finely chopped. Add remaining ingredients except pita bread. Process until smooth; chill at least 2 hours.

• Stir hummus before serving. If desired, add 1 to 2 tablespoons additional olive oil, or to taste. Serve with pita wedges.   *Makes 3½ cups dip*

Prep Time: 10 minutes
Chill Time: 2 hours

Creamy Artichoke-Parmesan Dip

Ginger-Lemon Cheese Spread with Pineapple-Peach Sauce

2 packages (8 ounces each) cream cheese, softened
1 cup sour cream
3 tablespoons packed brown sugar
1 tablespoon grated lemon peel
¾ teaspoon ground ginger
½ cup crushed pineapple, well drained
½ cup peach or apricot preserves
Assorted crackers and sliced fresh fruit, such as apples and pears

1. Line 3-cup decorative mold or bowl with plastic wrap.

2. Combine cream cheese and sour cream in large bowl; beat until creamy. (Do not overbeat.) Add brown sugar, lemon peel and ginger; stir until well blended.

3. Spoon cheese mixture into prepared mold. Cover with plastic wrap; refrigerate at least 8 hours or up to 2 days.

4. To complete recipe, combine pineapple and peach preserves in small bowl. Unmold cheese spread onto serving plate. Spoon sauce around cheese. Serve with crackers and fresh fruit. *Makes 8 servings*

Variation: Press toasted chopped walnuts onto cheese spread and serve Pineapple-Peach Sauce alongside of spread.

Make-Ahead Time: Up to 2 days before serving
Final Prep Time: 5 minutes

Ginger-Lemon Cheese Spread with Pineapple-Peach Sauce

Chutney Cheese Spread

2 packages (8 ounces each) fat-free cream cheese, softened
1 cup (4 ounces) shredded reduced-fat Cheddar cheese
½ cup mango chutney
¼ cup thinly sliced green onions with tops
3 tablespoons dark raisins, chopped
2 cloves garlic, minced
1 to 1½ teaspoons curry powder
¾ teaspoon ground coriander
½ to ¾ teaspoon ground ginger
1 tablespoon chopped dry roasted peanuts

1. Place cream cheese and Cheddar cheese in food processor or blender; process until smooth. Stir in chutney, green onions, raisins, garlic, curry powder, coriander and ginger. Cover; refrigerate 2 to 3 hours.

2. Top spread with peanuts. Serve with additional green onions and melba toast, if desired. *Makes 20 servings*

Variation: The spread may also be garnished with 1 tablespoon toasted coconut to provide a slightly sweeter flavor.

Herbed Garlic & Artichoke Dip

1 (6.5-ounce) package ALOUETTE® Garlic & Herbs or Light Garlic & Herbs
1 (15-ounce) can artichoke hearts, drained and chopped
½ cup minced green onions
2 tablespoons chopped sun-dried tomatoes
Freshly ground black pepper to taste

Preheat oven to 375°F.

Blend Alouette, artichokes, onions, tomatoes and pepper. Place cheese mixture in 2-cup oven-to-table dish; bake 10 to 12 minutes or until brown and bubbly. Serve warm with breadsticks, crackers or raw vegetables.

Makes 2 cups dip

Chutney Cheese Spread

Five-Layered Mexican Dip

½ cup low-fat sour cream
½ cup GUILTLESS GOURMET® Salsa (Roasted Red Pepper
    or Southwestern Grill)
1 jar (16 ounces) GUILTLESS GOURMET® Black Bean Dip
    (Spicy or Mild)
2 cups shredded lettuce
½ cup chopped tomato
¼ cup (1 ounce) shredded sharp Cheddar cheese
    Chopped fresh cilantro and cilantro sprigs (optional)
1 large bag (7 ounces) GUILTLESS GOURMET® Baked Tortilla
    Chips (yellow, white or blue corn)

Mix together sour cream and salsa in small bowl. Spread bean dip in shallow glass bowl. Top with sour cream-salsa mixture, spreading to cover bean dip.* Just before serving, top with lettuce, tomato and cheese. Garnish with cilantro, if desired. Serve with tortilla chips. *Makes 8 servings*

*Dip may be prepared to this point; cover and refrigerate up to 24 hours.

Chili Dip

1 container (16 ounces) sour cream
1 medium tomato, chopped (about 1 cup)
1 can (4 ounces) chopped green chilies, drained
1 package KNORR® Recipe Classics™ Leek Soup,
    Dip and Recipe Mix
3 to 4 teaspoons chili powder

● In medium bowl, combine all ingredients; chill at least 2 hours.

● Stir before serving. Serve with corn chips or cut-up vegetables.

Makes about 3 cups dip

Cheese Chili Dip: Stir in 1 cup shredded Monterey Jack cheese (about 4 ounces).

Variation: Use this dip to make Tortilla Roll-Ups. Simply spread Chili Dip on flour tortillas, top with cut-up cooked chicken, roll up and serve.

Prep Time: 5 minutes
Chill Time: 2 hours

Five-Layered Mexican Dip

Nutty Broccoli Spread

1 box (10 ounces) BIRDS EYE® frozen Chopped Broccoli
4 ounces cream cheese
¼ cup grated Parmesan cheese
1 teaspoon dried basil
¼ cup walnuts
1 loaf frozen garlic bread

• Cook broccoli according to package directions; drain well.

• Preheat oven to 400°F. Place broccoli, cream cheese, Parmesan cheese and basil in food processor or blender; process until ingredients are mixed. (Do not overmix.) Add walnuts; process 3 to 5 seconds.

• Split garlic bread lengthwise. Spread broccoli mixture evenly over bread.

• Bake 10 to 15 minutes or until bread is toasted and broccoli mixture is heated through.

• Cut bread into slices; serve hot. *Makes about 2 cups spread*

Prep Time: 10 minutes
Cook Time: 10 to 15 minutes

Two Cheese Pesto Dip

1 cup light sour cream
½ cup (2 ounces) SARGENTO® Light Mozzarella Shredded Cheese
½ cup light mayonnaise
½ cup finely chopped fresh parsley
¼ cup finely chopped walnuts
2 tablespoons SARGENTO® Fancy Parmesan Shredded Cheese
1½ teaspoons dried basil leaves *or* 3 tablespoons minced fresh basil
1 clove garlic, minced

Combine all ingredients in medium bowl. Cover and refrigerate several hours or overnight. Garnish with whole walnuts, if desired. Serve with assorted fresh vegetables. *Makes 2 cups dip*

Nutty Broccoli Spread

White Pizza Dip

1 envelope LIPTON® RECIPE SECRETS® Savory Herb
   with Garlic Soup Mix
1 container (16 ounces) sour cream
1 cup (8 ounces) ricotta cheese
1 cup shredded mozzarella cheese (about 4 ounces), divided
¼ cup (1 ounce) chopped pepperoni (optional)
1 loaf Italian or French bread, sliced

1. Preheat oven to 350°F. In shallow 1-quart casserole, combine soup mix, sour cream, ricotta cheese, ¾ cup mozzarella cheese and pepperoni.

2. Sprinkle with remaining ¼ cup mozzarella cheese.

3. Bake, uncovered, 30 minutes or until heated through. Serve with bread.

Makes 3 cups dip

Prep Time: 10 minutes
Cook Time: 30 minutes

Savory Peanut Butter Dip

¼ cup creamy peanut butter
3 ounces fat-free cream cheese
1 to 2 tablespoons lemon or apple juice
½ teaspoon ground cinnamon
⅛ to ¼ cup natural applesauce
2 apples, sliced
1 small banana, sliced
   Celery stalks, sliced into 4-inch pieces
2 cups broccoli flowerets

Combine the peanut butter, cream cheese, juice and cinnamon in food processor. Blend until smooth. Add applesauce, little by little, to bring to the desired consistency for the dip. Chill before serving with fresh fruits or vegetables.

Makes about 8 servings

*Favorite recipe from **Peanut Advisory Board***

White Pizza Dip

Celebration Cheese Ball

- **2 packages (8 ounces) cream cheese, softened**
- **⅓ cup mayonnaise**
- **¼ cup grated Parmesan cheese**
- **2 tablespoons finely chopped carrot**
- **1 tablespoon finely chopped red onion**
- **1½ teaspoons prepared horseradish**
- **¼ teaspoon salt**
- **½ cup chopped pecans or walnuts**
- **Assorted crackers and breadsticks**

Blend all ingredients except pecans and crackers in medium bowl. Cover and refrigerate until firm.

Form cheese mixture into a ball; roll in pecans. Wrap cheese ball in plastic wrap and refrigerate at least 1 hour. Serve with assorted crackers and breadsticks.

Makes about 2½ cups spread

Roasted Eggplant Dip

- **2 eggplants (about 1 pound each)**
- **¼ cup lemon juice**
- **3 tablespoons sesame tahini***
- **4 cloves garlic, minced**
- **2 teaspoons hot pepper sauce**
- **½ teaspoon salt**
- **Pita bread rounds, cut into wedges**

*Available in the ethnic section of the supermarket or in Middle Eastern grocery stores.

Prepare grill for direct cooking. Pierce eggplants in several places with fork. Place eggplants on grid. Grill, covered, over medium-high heat 30 to 40 minutes or until skin is black and blistered and pulp is soft, turning often. Peel eggplants when cool enough to handle. Let cool to room temperature.

Place eggplant pulp in food processor with lemon juice, tahini, garlic, pepper sauce and salt; process until smooth. Refrigerate at least 1 hour before serving to allow flavors to blend. Serve with pita bread wedges.

Makes 2 cups dip

Celebration Cheese Ball

CASUAL AFFAIRS

Maple-Glazed Meatballs

1½ **cups ketchup**
1 **cup maple syrup or maple-flavored syrup**
⅓ **cup reduced-sodium soy sauce**
1 **tablespoon quick-cooking tapioca**
1½ **teaspoons ground allspice**
1 **teaspoon dry mustard**
2 **packages (about 16 ounces each) frozen fully-cooked meatballs**
1 **can (20 ounces) pineapple chunks, drained**

SLOW COOKER DIRECTIONS

1. Stir together ketchup, syrup, soy sauce, tapioca, allspice and mustard in slow cooker.

2. Separate meatballs. Carefully stir meatballs and pineapple chunks into ketchup mixture. Cover; cook on LOW 5 to 6 hours. Stir before serving. Serve with cocktail picks. *Makes about 48 meatballs*

Prep Time: 10 minutes
Cook Time: 5 to 6 hours

Maple-Glazed Meatballs

Honey-Mustard Chicken Wings

3 pounds chicken wings
1 teaspoon salt
1 teaspoon black pepper
½ cup honey
½ cup barbecue sauce
2 tablespoons spicy brown mustard
1 clove garlic, minced
3 to 4 thin lemon slices

SLOW COOKER DIRECTIONS

1. Rinse chicken and pat dry. Cut off wing tips; discard. Cut each wing at joint to make two pieces. Sprinkle salt and pepper on both sides of chicken. Place wing pieces on broiler rack. Broil 4 to 5 inches from heat about 10 minutes, turning halfway through cooking. Place broiled chicken wings in slow cooker.

2. Combine honey, barbecue sauce, mustard and garlic in small bowl; mix well. Pour sauce over chicken wings. Top with lemon slices. Cover; cook on LOW 4 to 5 hours.

3. Remove and discard lemon slices. Serve wings with sauce.

Makes about 24 appetizers

Prep Time: 20 minutes
Cook Time: 4 to 5 hours

Sausage Cheese Puffs

1 pound BOB EVANS® Original Recipe Roll Sausage
2½ cups (10 ounces) shredded sharp Cheddar cheese
2 cups biscuit mix
½ cup water
1 teaspoon baking powder

Preheat oven to 350°F. Combine ingredients in large bowl until blended. Shape into 1-inch balls. Place on lightly greased baking sheets. Bake about 25 minutes or until golden brown. Serve hot. Refrigerate leftovers.

Makes about 60 appetizers

Honey-Mustard Chicken Wings

Tortilla Pizzettes

1 cup chunky salsa
1 cup refried beans
2 tablespoons chopped fresh cilantro
½ teaspoon ground cumin
3 large (10-inch) flour tortillas
1 cup (4 ounces) shredded Mexican cheese blend

Pour salsa into strainer; let drain at least 20 minutes.

Meanwhile, combine refried beans, cilantro and cumin in small bowl; mix well. Preheat oven to 400°F. Spray baking sheet lightly with nonstick cooking spray; set aside.

Cut each tortilla into 2½-inch circles with round cookie cutter (9 to 10 circles per tortilla). Spread each tortilla circle with refried bean mixture, leaving ¼ inch around edge. Top each with heaping teaspoon drained salsa; sprinkle with about 1 teaspoon cheese.

Place pizzettes on prepared baking sheet. Bake about 7 minutes or until tortillas are golden brown.   *Makes about 30 pizzettes*

Nacho Bacho

1½ pounds ground beef
1 cup chunky hot salsa
½ cup salad dressing
2 tablespoons Italian seasoning
1 tablespoon chili powder
2 cups (8 ounces) shredded Colby-Jack cheese, divided
3 cups nacho-flavored tortilla chips, crushed
1 cup sour cream
½ cup sliced black olives

Brown ground beef; drain. In medium bowl, combine salsa, salad dressing, Italian seasoning and chili powder. Add beef. Place in 11×7-inch baking dish. Top with 1 cup cheese. Cover with crushed chips and remaining 1 cup cheese. Bake at 350°F 20 minutes. Garnish with sour cream and sliced olives.

Makes 8 to 12 appetizer servings

*Favorite recipe from **North Dakota Beef Commission***

Tortilla Pizzettes

Easy Spinach Appetizer

- **2 tablespoons butter**
- **1 cup milk**
- **3 eggs**
- **1 cup all-purpose flour**
- **1 teaspoon baking powder**
- **1 teaspoon salt**
- **4 cups (16 ounces) shredded Monterey Jack cheese**
- **2 packages (10 ounces each) frozen chopped spinach, thawed and well drained**
- **½ cup diced red bell pepper**

Preheat oven to 350°F. Melt butter in 13×9-inch baking pan.

Beat milk, eggs, flour, baking powder and salt in medium bowl until well blended. Stir in cheese, spinach and bell pepper; mix well. Spread mixture over melted butter in pan.

Bake 40 to 45 minutes or until firm. Let stand 10 minutes before cutting into triangles or squares.   *Makes 2 to 4 dozen pieces*

TIP This tasty appetizer can be made ahead, frozen and reheated. After baking, cool completely and cut into squares. Transfer the squares to a baking sheet; place it in the freezer until the squares are frozen solid. Then transfer the squares to a resealable food storage bag. Seal it tightly and store it in the freezer. To serve, reheat the squares in a preheated 325°F oven for 15 minutes.

Easy Spinach Appetizer

Cheesy Snack Squares

1¼ cups all-purpose flour
¾ cup cornmeal
2 medium green onions, thinly sliced
4 teaspoons sugar
2 teaspoons baking powder
1 teaspoon dried Italian seasoning
¼ teaspoon salt
1 cup milk
¼ cup vegetable oil
1 egg
1 cup (4 ounces) shredded Cheddar cheese
¼ cup finely chopped green bell pepper
¼ cup finely chopped red bell pepper
2 slices crisp-cooked bacon, crumbled

Preheat oven to 400°F. Grease 11×7-inch baking dish.

Combine flour, cornmeal, green onions, sugar, baking powder, Italian seasoning and salt in large bowl; mix well. Combine milk, oil and egg in small bowl. Add to cornmeal mixture; mix just until moistened. Spread evenly in prepared dish. Combine cheese, bell peppers and bacon in medium bowl. Sprinkle evenly over cornmeal mixture.

Bake 25 to 30 minutes or until wooden toothpick inserted into center comes out clean. Let stand 10 minutes before cutting.

Makes about 15 appetizers

Cheesy Snack Squares

Chicken Pesto Pizza

1 loaf (1 pound) frozen bread dough, thawed
8 ounces chicken tenders, cut into ½-inch pieces
½ red onion, cut into quarters and thinly sliced
¼ cup prepared pesto
2 large plum tomatoes, seeded and diced
1 cup (4 ounces) shredded pizza cheese blend or
   mozzarella cheese

Preheat oven to 375°F. Roll out bread dough on floured surface to 14×8-inch rectangle. Transfer to baking sheet sprinkled with cornmeal. Cover loosely with plastic wrap and let rise 20 to 30 minutes.

Meanwhile, spray large skillet with nonstick cooking spray; heat over medium heat. Add chicken; cook and stir 2 minutes. Add onion and pesto; cook and stir 3 to 4 minutes or until chicken is cooked through. Stir in tomatoes; remove from heat and let cool slightly.

Spread chicken mixture evenly over bread dough to within 1 inch of edges. Sprinkle with cheese.

Bake on bottom rack of oven about 20 minutes or until crust is golden brown. Cut into 2-inch squares. *Makes about 20 appetizer pieces*

Original Ranch® Drummettes

1 packet (1 ounce) HIDDEN VALLEY® The Original Ranch®
   Salad Dressing & Seasoning Mix
¼ cup vegetable oil
24 chicken drummettes (about 2 pounds)

Combine dressing mix and oil in large bowl. Add drummettes; toss well to coat. Arrange on rack placed in foil-lined baking pan; bake at 425°F for 25 minutes. Turn drummettes over; bake additional 20 minutes.

Makes 24 drummettes

Spicy Hot Variation: Add 2 tablespoons red pepper sauce to dressing mixture before coating.

Serving Suggestion: Dip cooked drummettes in prepared Hidden Valley® Original Ranch® Salad Dressing.

Chicken Pesto Pizza

Cheese & Sausage Bundles

Salsa (recipe follows)
¼ **pound bulk hot Italian pork sausage**
1 **cup (4 ounces) shredded Monterey Jack cheese**
1 **can (4 ounces) chopped green chilies**
2 **tablespoons finely chopped green onion**
40 **wonton wrappers**
1 **quart vegetable oil for deep frying**

1. Prepare Salsa; set aside and keep warm. Brown sausage in small skillet over medium-high heat 6 to 8 minutes, stirring to separate meat. Drain off drippings. Combine sausage, cheese, chilies and onion in medium bowl. Spoon 1 round teaspoon sausage mixture near 1 corner of wonton wrapper. Brush opposite corner with water. Fold over corner; roll up jelly-roll style.

2. Moisten ends of roll with water. Bring ends together to make a "bundle," overlapping ends slightly; firmly press to seal. Repeat with remaining filling and wonton wrappers.

3. Heat oil in heavy 3-quart saucepan over medium heat until deep-fat thermometer registers 365°F. Fry bundles, a few at a time, about 1½ minutes or until golden. Adjust heat to maintain temperature. (Allow oil to return to 365°F between batches.) Drain on paper towels. Serve with Salsa.

Makes 40 appetizers

Salsa

1 **can (16 ounces) whole tomatoes, undrained**
2 **tablespoons olive oil**
2 **tablespoons chopped green onion**
2 **cloves garlic, minced**
3 **tablespoons chopped fresh cilantro or parsley**

Combine tomatoes with juice and oil in food processor; process until chopped. Pour into 1-quart saucepan. Stir in green onion and garlic. Bring to a boil over medium heat. Cook, uncovered, 5 minutes. Remove from heat. Stir in cilantro.

Makes 1¾ cups salsa

Cheese & Sausage Bundles

PARTY PICK-UPS

Mini Chickpea Cakes

1 can (15 ounces) chickpeas, rinsed and drained
1 cup shredded carrots
⅓ cup seasoned dry bread crumbs
¼ cup creamy Italian salad dressing
1 egg

1. Preheat oven to 375°F. Spray baking sheets with nonstick cooking spray.

2. Mash chickpeas coarsely in medium bowl with potato masher. Stir in carrots, bread crumbs, salad dressing and egg; mix well.

3. Shape chickpea mixture into small patties, using about 1 tablespoon mixture for each. Place on prepared baking sheets.

4. Bake 15 to 18 minutes, turning halfway through baking time, until chickpea cakes are lightly browned on both sides. Serve warm with additional salad dressing for dipping, if desired.

Makes about 2 dozen appetizers

Mini Chickpea Cakes

Party Stuffed Pinwheels

1 envelope LIPTON® RECIPE SECRETS® Savory Herb with Garlic Soup Mix*

1 package (8 ounces) cream cheese, softened

1 cup shredded mozzarella cheese (about 4 ounces)

2 tablespoons milk

1 tablespoon grated Parmesan cheese

2 packages (10 ounces each) refrigerated pizza crust

Also terrific with LIPTON® RECIPE SECRETS® Onion Soup Mix.

1. Preheat oven to 425°F. In medium bowl, combine all ingredients except pizza crusts; set aside.

2. Unroll pizza crusts, then top evenly with filling. Roll, starting at longest side, jelly-roll style. Cut each roll into 16 rounds.**

3. On baking sheet sprayed with nonstick cooking spray, arrange rounds cut side down.

4. Bake, uncovered, 13 minutes or until golden brown.

Makes 32 pinwheels

If rolled pizza crust is too soft to cut, refrigerate or freeze until firm.

TIP **To simplify last minute preparation, make the Pinwheel filling ahead of time and refrigerate. Bring the filling to room temperature before spreading over the crust.**

Party Stuffed Pinwheels

Chicken Empanadas

4 **ounces cream cheese**
2 **tablespoons chopped fresh cilantro**
2 **tablespoons salsa**
½ **teaspoon salt**
½ **teaspoon ground cumin**
¼ **teaspoon garlic powder**
1 **cup finely chopped cooked chicken**
1 **box (15 ounces) refrigerated pie crusts (two 11-inch rounds), at room temperature**
1 **egg, beaten**
  Additional salsa

1. Heat cream cheese in small heavy saucepan over low heat; cook and stir until melted. Add cilantro, salsa, salt, cumin and garlic powder; stir until smooth. Stir in chicken; remove from heat.

2. Roll out pie crust dough slightly on lightly floured surface. Cut dough with 3-inch round cookie or biscuit cutter. Reroll dough scraps and cut enough additional to make 20 rounds.

3. Preheat oven to 425°F. Line 2 baking sheets with parchment paper or foil. Place about 2 teaspoons chicken mixture in center of each round. Brush edges lightly with water. Pull one side of dough over filling to form half circle; pinch edges to seal.

4. Place 10 empanadas on each prepared baking sheet; brush lightly with egg. Bake 16 to 18 minutes or until lightly brown. Serve with salsa.

Makes 20 empanadas

TIP **Empanadas can be prepared ahead of time and frozen. Simply wrap unbaked empanadas with plastic wrap and freeze. Follow directions above and bake 18 to 20 minutes.**

Chicken Empanadas

Festive Taco Cups

1 tablespoon vegetable oil
½ cup chopped onion
½ pound ground turkey or ground beef
1 clove garlic, minced
½ teaspoon dried oregano leaves
½ teaspoon chili powder or taco seasoning
¼ teaspoon salt
1¼ cups shredded taco-flavored cheese or Mexican cheese blend, divided
1 can (11½ ounces) refrigerated corn breadstick dough
Chopped fresh tomato and sliced green onion for garnish (optional)

1. Heat oil in large skillet over medium heat. Add onion and cook until tender. Add turkey; cook until turkey is no longer pink, stirring occasionally. Stir in garlic, oregano, chili powder and salt. Remove from heat and stir in ½ cup cheese; set aside.

2. Preheat oven to 375°F. Lightly grease 36 miniature (1¾-inch) muffin pan cups. Remove dough from container but do not unroll dough. Separate dough into 8 pieces at perforations. Divide each piece into 3 pieces; roll or pat each piece into 3-inch circle. Press circles into prepared muffin pan cups.

3. Fill each cup with 1½ to 2 teaspoons turkey mixture. Bake 10 minutes. Sprinkle tops of taco cups with remaining ¾ cup cheese; bake 2 to 3 minutes more until cheese is melted. Garnish with tomato and green onion, if desired.

Makes 36 taco cups

Festive Taco Cups

Mushrooms Rockefeller

18 large fresh button mushrooms (about 1 pound)
2 slices bacon
¼ cup chopped onion
1 package (10 ounces) frozen chopped spinach, thawed and squeezed dry
1 tablespoon lemon juice
1 teaspoon grated lemon peel
½ jar (2 ounces) chopped pimiento, drained
Lemon slices for garnish

1. Lightly spray 13×9-inch baking dish with nonstick cooking spray. Preheat oven to 375°F. Brush dirt from mushrooms; clean by wiping mushrooms with damp paper towel. Pull entire stem out of each mushroom cap.

2. Cut thin slice from base of each stem; discard. Chop stems.

3. Cook bacon in medium skillet over medium heat until crisp. Remove bacon with tongs to paper towel; set aside. Add mushroom stems and onion to hot drippings in skillet. Cook and stir until onion is soft. Add spinach, lemon juice, lemon peel and pimiento; blend well. Stuff mushroom caps with spinach mixture; place in single layer in prepared baking dish. Crumble reserved bacon and sprinkle on top of mushrooms. Bake 15 minutes or until heated through. Garnish, if desired. Serve immediately.

Makes 18 appetizers

Mushrooms Rockefeller

Antipasto Crescent Bites

2 ounces cream cheese (do not use reduced-fat or fat-free cream cheese)
1 package (8 ounces) refrigerated crescent roll dough
1 egg plus 1 tablespoon water, beaten
4 strips roasted red pepper, cut into 3×¾-inch-long strips
2 large marinated artichoke hearts, cut in half lengthwise to ¾-inch width
1 thin slice Genoa or other salami, cut into 4 strips
4 small stuffed green olives, cut into halves

1. Preheat oven to 375°F. Cut cream cheese into 16 equal pieces, about 1 teaspoon per piece; set aside. Remove dough from package. Unroll on lightly floured surface. Cut each triangle of dough in half to form 2 triangles. Brush outer edges of triangle lightly with egg mixture.

2. Wrap 1 pepper strip around 1 piece of cream cheese. Place on dough triangle. Fold over and pinch edges to seal; repeat with remaining pepper strips. Place 1 piece artichoke heart and 1 piece of cream cheese on dough triangle. Fold over and pinch edges to seal; repeat with remaining pieces of artichoke hearts. Wrap 1 strip salami around 1 piece of cream cheese. Place on dough triangle. Fold over and pinch edges to seal; repeat with remaining salami. Place 2 olive halves and 1 piece of cream cheese on dough triangle. Fold over and pinch edges to seal; repeat with remaining olives. Place on ungreased baking sheet. Brush with egg mixture.

3. Bake 12 to 14 minutes or until golden brown. Cool on wire rack. Store in airtight container in refrigerator.

4. Reheat on baking sheet in preheated 325°F oven 7 to 8 minutes or until warmed through. Do not microwave. *Makes 16 pieces*

Antipasto Crescent Bites

Quick Sausage Appetizers

½ pound BOB EVANS® Italian Roll Sausage
⅓ cup mozzarella cheese
¼ cup sour cream
3 tablespoons mayonnaise
2 tablespoons chopped green onion
½ teaspoon Worcestershire sauce
10 slices white bread*

Party rye or thinly sliced French bread can be used instead of white bread. Double recipe to have enough sausage mixture.

Preheat broiler. Crumble and cook sausage in medium skillet until browned. Drain on paper towels. Transfer sausage to small bowl; stir in cheese, sour cream, mayonnaise, green onion and Worcestershire. Cut crusts from bread. Cut each slice into 4 squares; spread about 1 teaspoon sausage mixture onto each square. Arrange squares on ungreased baking sheet; place under hot broiler just until cheese melts and topping bubbles. (Be careful not to burn corners and edges.) Serve hot.   *Makes 40 appetizer squares*

TIP **Quick Sausage Appetizers may be made ahead and refrigerated overnight or frozen up to 1 month before broiling.**

Quick Sausage Appetizers

FESTIVE FLAIR

Spinach Cheese Bundles

1 container (6½ ounces) garlic- and herb-flavored spreadable cheese
½ cup chopped fresh spinach
¼ teaspoon black pepper
1 package (17¼ ounces) frozen puff pastry dough, thawed
Sweet and sour or favorite dipping sauce (optional)

1. Preheat oven to 400°F. Combine cheese, spinach and pepper in small bowl; mix well.

2. Roll out one sheet dough on floured surface into 12-inch square. Cut into 16 (3-inch) squares. Place about 1 teaspoon cheese mixture in center of each square; brush edges of squares with water. Bring edges together up over filling and twist tightly to seal; fan out corners of puff pastry. Repeat with remaining sheet of puff pastry and cheese mixture.

3. Place bundles 2 inches apart on ungreased baking sheets. Bake about 13 minutes or until golden brown. Serve warm with dipping sauce, if desired. *Makes 32 bundles*

Spinach Cheese Bundles

Pesto Cheesecake

CRUST
- 1 cup fine dry bread crumbs
- ½ cup very finely chopped toasted pine nuts or walnuts
- 3 tablespoons melted butter or margarine

FILLING
- 2 cups (15 ounces) SARGENTO® Light Ricotta Cheese
- ½ cup half-and-half
- 2 tablespoons all-purpose flour
- ½ teaspoon salt
- 2 eggs
- ⅓ cup Homemade Pesto Sauce (recipe follows) or prepared pesto sauce

Preheat oven to 350°F. Lightly grease sides of 8- or 9-inch springform pan.

Combine bread crumbs, nuts and butter in small bowl until well blended. Press evenly onto bottom of pan. Refrigerate until ready to use.

Combine Ricotta cheese, half-and-half, flour and salt in medium bowl with electric mixer. Beat at medium speed until smooth. Add eggs, one at a time; beat until smooth. Pour into prepared crust. Spoon pesto by teaspoonsful randomly over cheese mixture. Gently swirl with knife for marbled effect.

Bake 45 minutes or until center is just set; turn off oven. Cool in oven with door open 30 minutes. Remove from oven. Cool completely on wire rack. Cut into thin slices before serving. *Makes 10 servings*

Homemade Pesto Sauce: In food processor or blender, mince 1 clove garlic. Add ½ cup packed fresh basil leaves and 1 tablespoon toasted pine nuts or walnuts. Process until smooth, scraping down side of bowl once. With machine running, drizzle 2 tablespoons olive oil into bowl; process until smooth. Add ¼ cup (1 ounce) SARGENTO® Fancy Parmesan Shredded Cheese; process just until cheese is blended.

Pesto Cheesecake

Pepper Cheese Cocktail Puffs

½ package (17¼ ounces) frozen puff pastry dough, thawed
1 tablespoon Dijon mustard
½ cup (2 ounces) finely shredded Cheddar cheese
1 teaspoon cracked black pepper
1 egg
1 tablespoon water

1. Preheat oven to 400°F. Grease baking sheets.

2. Roll out 1 sheet puff pastry dough on well floured surface to 14×10-inch rectangle. Spread half of dough (from 10-inch side) with mustard. Sprinkle with cheese and pepper. Fold dough over filling; roll gently to seal edges.

3. Cut lengthwise into 3 strips; cut each strip diagonally into 1½-inch pieces. Place on prepared baking sheets. Beat egg and water in small bowl; brush on appetizers.

4. Bake appetizers 12 to 15 minutes or until puffed and deep golden brown. Remove from baking sheets to wire rack to cool.

Makes about 20 appetizers

Prep and Bake Time: 30 minutes

TIP **For the best puffs, work quickly and efficiently with the puff pastry. The colder puff pastry is, the better it will puff in the hot oven. Double this recipe for tasty bites that will be gone before the oven is cool.**

Pepper Cheese Cocktail Puffs

Cranberry-Walnut Pear Wedges

3 firm ripe pears, cut into quarters and cored
¼ cup triple sec*
2 tablespoons orange juice
½ cup prepared cranberry fruit relish
¼ cup finely chopped walnuts
¼ cup (1 ounce) crumbled blue cheese

*Omit liqueur, if desired. Increase orange juice to ¼ cup. Add 2 tablespoons honey and 2 tablespoons balsamic vinegar to marinade.

1. Place pears in resealable food storage bag. Pour liqueur and orange juice over pears; seal bag. Turn bag over several times to coat pears evenly. Refrigerate at least 1 hour, turning bag occasionally.

2. Drain pears; discard marinade. Place pears on serving platter. Spoon cranberry relish evenly into cavities of pears; sprinkle with walnuts and cheese. Garnish, if desired. *Makes 12 servings*

Brie Torte

1 (15- to 16-ounce) wheel Brie cheese
6 tablespoons butter, softened
⅓ cup chopped dried tart cherries
¼ cup finely chopped pecans
½ teaspoon dried thyme *or* 2 teaspoons finely chopped fresh thyme

Refrigerate Brie until chilled and firm or freeze 30 minutes until firm. Cut Brie in half horizontally.

Combine butter, cherries, pecans and thyme in small bowl; mix well. Spread mixture evenly onto cut side of one half of Brie. Top with other half, cut side down. Lightly press together. Wrap in plastic wrap; refrigerate 1 to 2 hours. To serve, cut into serving size wedges and bring to room temperature. Serve with water crackers. *Makes about 20 appetizer servings*

Note: If wrapped securely in plastic wrap, this appetizer will keep in the refrigerator for at least one week.

*Favorite recipe from **Cherry Marketing Institute***

PARTY FOOD

Contents

Appetizers & Snacks

Roasted Red Potato Bites

1½ pounds red potatoes (about 15 small)
  1 cup shredded cheddar cheese (about 4 ounces)
  ½ cup HELLMANN'S® or BEST FOODS® Real Mayonnaise
  ½ cup sliced green onions
  2 tablespoons chopped fresh basil leaves (optional)
 10 slices bacon, crisp-cooked and crumbled

1. Preheat oven to 400°F. On large baking sheet, arrange potatoes and bake 35 minutes or until tender. Let stand until cool enough to handle.

2. Cut each potato in half, then cut thin slice from bottom of each potato half. With small melon baller or spoon, scoop pulp from potatoes leaving ¼-inch shell. Place pulp in medium bowl; set shells shells aside.

3. In medium bowl, lightly mash reserved pulp. Stir in remaining ingredients. Spoon or pipe potato filling into potato shells.

4. Arrange filled shells on baking sheet and broil 3 minutes or until golden and heated through. *Makes 30 bites*

Prep Time: 10 minutes
Cook Time: 40 minutes

Roasted Red Potato Bites

Festive Chicken Dip

1½ pounds boneless, skinless chicken breasts, finely chopped
    (about 3 cups)
¼ cup lime juice, divided
2 cloves garlic, minced
1 teaspoon salt
½ teaspoon ground black pepper
1 can (16 ounces) refried beans
1½ cups sour cream, divided
1 package (1¼ ounces) dry taco seasoning mix, divided
1 tablespoon picante sauce
1 avocado, chopped
1 tablespoon olive oil
1 cup (4 ounces) shredded sharp Cheddar cheese
1 small onion, finely chopped
2 tomatoes, finely chopped
1 can (2¼ ounces) sliced black olives, drained and chopped
1 bag (10 ounces) tortilla chips
    Fresh cilantro for garnish

Place chicken in small bowl. Sprinkle with 3 tablespoons lime juice, garlic, salt and pepper; mix well. Set aside. Combine beans, ½ cup sour cream, 2½ tablespoons taco seasoning mix and picante sauce in medium bowl. Spread bean mixture on bottom of shallow 2-quart casserole dish. Combine avocado and remaining 1 tablespoon lime juice in small bowl; sprinkle over bean mixture. Combine remaining 1 cup sour cream and 2½ tablespoons taco seasoning mix in small bowl; set aside. Heat oil in large skillet over high heat until hot; add chicken in single layer. Do not stir. Cook about 2 minutes or until chicken is brown on bottom. Turn chicken and cook until other side is brown and no liquid remains. Break chicken into separate pieces with fork. Layer chicken, sour cream mixture, cheese, onion and tomatoes over avocado mixture. Top with olives. Refrigerate until completely chilled. Serve with chips. Garnish with cilantro.

Makes 2 quarts dip (about 30 appetizer servings)

Favorite recipe from **National Chicken Council**

Festive Chicken Dip

Barbecued Swedish Meatballs

Meatballs
1½ pounds lean ground beef
1 cup finely chopped onion
½ cup fresh breadcrumbs
½ cup HOLLAND HOUSE® White Cooking Wine
1 egg, beaten
½ teaspoon ground allspice
½ teaspoon ground nutmeg
Sauce
1 jar (10 ounces) currant jelly
½ cup chili sauce
¼ cup HOLLAND HOUSE® White Cooking Wine
1 tablespoon cornstarch

Heat oven to 350°F. In medium bowl, combine all meatball ingredients; mix well. Shape into 1-inch balls. Place meatballs in 15×10×1-inch baking pan. Bake 20 minutes or until brown.

In medium saucepan, combine all sauce ingredients; mix well. Cook over medium heat until mixture boils and thickens, stirring occasionally. Add meatballs. To serve, place meatballs and sauce in fondue pot or chafing dish.   *Makes 6 to 8 servings*

Sausage Pinwheels

2 cups biscuit mix
½ cup milk
¼ cup butter or margarine, melted
1 pound BOB EVANS® Original Recipe Roll Sausage

Combine biscuit mix, milk and butter in large bowl until blended. Refrigerate 30 minutes. Divide dough into two portions. Roll out one portion on floured surface to ⅛-inch-thick rectangle, about 10×7 inches. Spread with half the sausage. Roll lengthwise into long roll. Repeat with remaining dough and sausage. Place rolls in freezer until firm enough to cut easily. Preheat oven to 400°F. Cut rolls into thin slices. Place on baking sheets. Bake 15 minutes or until golden brown. Serve hot. Refrigerate leftovers.   *Makes 48 pinwheels*

Note: This recipe can be doubled. Refreeze after slicing. When ready to serve, thaw slices in refrigerator and bake.

Barbecued Swedish Meatballs

Crostini

¼ **loaf whole wheat baguette (4 ounces)**
4 **plum tomatoes**
1 **cup (4 ounces) shredded part-skim mozzarella cheese**
3 **tablespoons prepared pesto sauce**

1. Preheat oven to 400°F. Slice baguette into 16 very thin, diagonal slices. Slice each tomato vertically into four ¼-inch slices.

2. Place baguette slices on ungreased nonstick baking sheet. Top each with 1 tablespoon cheese and 1 slice tomato. Bake about 8 minutes or until bread is lightly toasted and cheese is melted. Top each crostini with about ½ teaspoon pesto sauce. Serve warm.

Makes 16 appetizers

Hidden Valley® Torta

2 **packages (8 ounces each) cream cheese, softened**
1 **packet (1 ounce) HIDDEN VALLEY® The Original Ranch® Salad Dressing & Seasoning Mix**
1 **jar (6 ounces) marinated artichoke hearts, drained and chopped**
⅓ **cup roasted red peppers, drained and chopped**
3 **tablespoons minced fresh parsley**

Beat cream cheese and salad dressing & seasoning mix together in a medium bowl. In a separate bowl, stir together artichokes, peppers and parsley. In a 3-cup bowl lined with plastic wrap, alternate layers of cream cheese mixture and vegetable mixture, beginning and ending with a cheese layer.

Chill 4 hours or overnight. Invert onto plate; remove plastic wrap. Serve with crackers.

Makes 10 to 12 servings

Crostini

Mini Pizzas

Crust
   ⅓ **cup olive oil**
   1 **tablespoon TABASCO® brand Pepper Sauce**
   2 **large cloves garlic, minced**
   1 **teaspoon dried rosemary, crumbled**
   1 **(16-ounce) package hot roll mix with yeast packet**
1¼ **cups hot water**
Goat Cheese Topping
   1 **large tomato, diced**
   ¼ **cup crumbled goat cheese**
   2 **tablespoons chopped fresh parsley**
Roasted Pepper and Olive Topping
   ½ **cup shredded mozzarella cheese**
   ½ **cup pitted green olives**
   ⅓ **cup roasted red pepper strips**
Artichoke Topping
   ½ **cup chopped artichoke hearts**
   ½ **cup cherry tomatoes, sliced into wedges**
   ⅓ **cup sliced green onions**

For crust, combine olive oil, TABASCO® Sauce, garlic and rosemary
in small bowl. Combine hot roll mix, yeast packet, hot water and
2 tablespoons oil mixture in large bowl; stir until dough pulls away from
side of bowl. Turn dough onto lightly floured surface; shape into ball.
Knead until smooth, adding additional flour as necessary.

Preheat oven to 425°F. For toppings, combine ingredients in separate
bowls. Cut dough into quarters; cut each quarter into 10 equal pieces.
Roll each piece into ball. Press each ball into 2-inch round on large
cookie sheet; brush each round with remaining oil mixture. Arrange
about 2 teaspoons topping on each dough round. Bake 12 minutes or
until dough is lightly browned and puffed.   *Makes 40 appetizers*

Mini Pizzas

Crab and Artichoke Stuffed Mushrooms

½ pound Florida blue crab meat
1 (14-ounce) can artichoke hearts, drained and finely chopped
1 cup mayonnaise*
½ cup grated Parmesan cheese
¼ teaspoon lemon pepper seasoning
⅛ teaspoon salt
⅛ teaspoon cayenne pepper
30 large fresh Florida mushrooms

Or, you can substitute mixture of ½ cup mayonnaise and ½ cup plain yogurt.

Remove any pieces of shell or cartilage from crab meat. Combine crab meat, artichoke hearts, mayonnaise, Parmesan cheese and seasonings; mix until well blended. Remove stems from mushrooms and fill the caps with crab meat mixture. Place in a lightly greased, shallow baking dish. Bake in a preheated 400°F oven for 10 minutes or until hot and bubbly.   *Makes 30 appetizer servings*

Favorite recipe from **Florida Department of Agriculture and Consumer Services, Bureau of Seafood and Aquaculture**

Easy Italian No-Bake Snack Mix

3 tablespoons olive oil
1 tablespoon dried Italian seasoning
1 box (7 ounces) baked crispy snack crackers
4 cups small bow tie pretzels
1 can (12 ounces) cocktail peanuts
¼ cup grated Parmesan cheese

1. Combine oil and seasoning in large resealable food storage bag; knead well.

2. Add crackers, pretzels and peanuts. Seal bag; shake gently to coat well with oil mixture. Add cheese. Seal bag; shake gently to coat evenly. Snack mix can be stored in bag up to 5 days.

Makes 10 cups snack mix

Prep Time: 10 minutes

Crab and Artichoke Stuffed Mushrooms

Chile 'n' Cheese Spirals

    4 ounces cream cheese, softened
    1 cup (4 ounces) shredded cheddar cheese
    1 can (4 ounces) ORTEGA® Diced Green Chiles
    3 green onions, sliced
    ½ cup chopped red bell pepper
    1 can (2.25 ounces) chopped ripe olives
    4 (8-inch) taco-size flour tortillas
      ORTEGA Salsa (any flavor)

COMBINE cream cheese, cheddar cheese, chiles, green onions, pepper and olives in medium bowl.

SPREAD ½ cup cheese mixture on each tortilla; roll up. Wrap each roll in plastic wrap; chill for 1 hour.

REMOVE plastic wrap; slice each roll into six ¾-inch pieces. Serve with salsa for dipping.   *Makes 24 appetizers*

Tip: Chili 'n' Cheese Spirals can be made ahead and kept in the refrigerator for 1 to 2 days.

Smoked Salmon Roses

     1 package (8 ounces) cream cheese, softened
     1 tablespoon prepared horseradish
     1 tablespoon minced fresh dill plus whole sprigs
     1 tablespoon half-and-half
    16 slices (12 to 16 ounces) smoked salmon
     1 red bell pepper, cut into thin strips

1. Combine cream cheese, horseradish, minced dill and half-and-half in small bowl. Beat until light and creamy.

2. Spread 1 tablespoon cream cheese mixture over each salmon slice. Roll up jelly-roll fashion. Slice each roll in half crosswise. Arrange salmon rolls, cut sides down, on serving dish to resemble roses. Garnish each "rose" by tucking 1 pepper strip and 1 dill sprig in center.

                Makes 32 servings

Chile 'n' Cheese Spirals

Spinach-Artichoke Party Cups

Nonstick cooking spray
36 (3-inch) wonton wrappers
1 can (8½ ounces) artichoke hearts, drained and chopped
½ (10-ounce) package frozen chopped spinach, thawed and squeezed dry
1 cup shredded Monterey Jack cheese
½ cup grated Parmesan cheese
½ cup mayonnaise
1 clove garlic, minced

1. Preheat oven to 300°F. Spray miniature (1¾-inch) muffin pan cups lightly with cooking spray. Press 1 wonton wrapper into each cup; spray lightly with cooking spray. Bake about 9 minutes or until light golden brown. Remove shells from pan; place on wire rack to cool. Repeat with remaining wonton wrappers.*

2. Meanwhile, combine artichoke hearts, spinach, cheeses, mayonnaise and garlic in medium bowl; mix well.

3. Fill each wonton cup with about 1½ teaspoons spinach-artichoke mixture. Place filled cups on baking sheet. Bake about 7 minutes or until heated through. Serve immediately.   *Makes 36 appetizers*

Wonton cups may be prepared up to one week in advance. Cool completely and store in an airtight container.

Tip: If you have leftover spinach-artichoke mixture after filling the wonton cups, place the mixture in a shallow ovenproof dish and bake it at 350°F until hot and bubbly. Serve it with bread or crackers.

Spinach-Artichoke Party Cups

Salads & Sides

Spicy Chickpeas & Couscous

- 1 can (about 14 ounces) vegetable broth
- 1 teaspoon ground coriander
- ½ teaspoon ground cardamom
- ½ teaspoon ground turmeric
- ½ teaspoon hot pepper sauce
- ¼ teaspoon salt
- ⅛ teaspoon ground cinnamon
- 1 cup matchstick-size carrots
- 1 can (15 ounces) chickpeas, rinsed and drained
- 1 cup frozen green peas
- 1 cup quick-cooking couscous
- 2 tablespoons chopped fresh mint or parsley

1. Combine vegetable broth, coriander, cardamom, turmeric, pepper sauce, salt and cinnamon in large saucepan; bring to a boil over high heat. Add carrots; reduce heat and simmer 5 minutes.

2. Add chickpeas and green peas; return to a simmer. Simmer, uncovered, about 2 minutes.

3. Stir in couscous. Cover; remove from heat. Let stand 5 minutes or until liquid is absorbed. Sprinkle with mint.   *Makes 6 servings*

Spicy Chickpeas & Couscous

Broccoli-Cheese Pilaf

¼ cup minced onion
¼ cup diced red bell pepper
2 cups instant rice
1⅓ cups water
1 can (10¾ ounces) condensed broccoli and cheese soup, undiluted
1 tablespoon minced fresh parsley
½ teaspoon salt

1. Lightly coat medium saucepan with nonstick cooking spray. Add onion and pepper; cook and stir until tender.

2. Stir in rice; add water, soup, parsley and salt. Mix well.

3. Bring to a boil. Reduce heat; cover and cook 10 minutes or until liquid is absorbed and rice is tender.   *Makes 6 servings*

Ranch Picnic Potato Salad

6 medium potatoes (about 3½ pounds), cooked, peeled and sliced
½ cup chopped celery
¼ cup sliced green onions
2 tablespoons chopped fresh parsley
1 teaspoon salt
⅛ teaspoon black pepper
1 cup HIDDEN VALLEY® The Original Ranch® Dressing
1 tablespoon Dijon mustard
2 hard-cooked eggs, finely chopped
Paprika
Lettuce (optional)

Combine potatoes, celery, onions, parsley, salt and pepper in a large bowl. Stir together dressing and mustard in a small bowl; pour over potato mixture and toss lightly. Cover and refrigerate several hours. Sprinkle with eggs and paprika. Serve in a lettuce-lined bowl, if desired.

Makes 8 servings

Broccoli-Cheese Pilaf

Pasta Salad with Pesto

1 package BOB EVANS® Italian Grillin' Sausage (approximately
   5 links)
1 pound uncooked penne pasta
1 tablespoon butter or margarine
2 cloves garlic, peeled
2 cups fresh basil leaves
½ cup fresh parsley leaves
2 tablespoons pine nuts
½ cup olive oil
¼ cup freshly grated Parmesan cheese
¼ teaspoon black pepper
2 cups seeded and diced Roma tomatoes
1 small green bell pepper, chopped
1 cup pitted whole ripe olives
1 cup (4 ounces) cubed mozzarella cheese
   Red leaf lettuce for garnish (optional)

Cook sausage in large skillet or on grill until browned; let cool. Cut in half lengthwise; cut each half into ¼-inch slices and set aside.

Cook penne according to package directions; drain. Toss in large bowl with butter to prevent sticking.

To prepare pesto sauce, place garlic in food processor with metal blade or in blender; process until smooth. Add basil and parsley; process until finely chopped. Add pine nuts; process until finely chopped. With motor running, slowly add olive oil in fine, steady stream. Add Parmesan cheese and black pepper; process until well blended, scraping down side as needed.

To assemble salad, toss sausage, tomatoes, bell pepper, olives and mozzarella cheese with penne. Gradually stir in pesto until salad is moist but not saturated. Serve salad on lettuce-lined platter, if desired. Refrigerate leftovers. *Makes 8 servings*

Pasta Salad with Pesto

Marinated Bean and Vegetable Salad

¼ **cup orange juice**
3 **tablespoons white wine vinegar**
1 **tablespoon canola or vegetable oil**
2 **cloves garlic, minced**
1 **can (15 ounces) Great Northern beans, rinsed and drained**
1 **can (15 ounces) kidney beans, rinsed and drained**
¼ **cup coarsely chopped red cabbage**
¼ **cup chopped red onion**
¼ **cup chopped green bell pepper**
¼ **cup chopped red bell pepper**
¼ **cup sliced celery**

1. For dressing, combine orange juice, vinegar, oil and garlic in small jar with tight-fitting lid; shake well.

2. Combine beans, cabbage, onion, bell peppers and celery in large bowl. Pour dressing over bean mixture; toss to coat.

3. Refrigerate, covered, 1 to 2 hours to allow flavors to blend. Toss before serving.   *Makes 8 servings*

Cool Summer Gazpacho Salad

3 **cups fresh DOLE® Tropical Gold® Pineapple, cut into chunks**
2 **cups chopped tomatoes, drained**
1 **large cucumber, halved lengthwise and thinly sliced**
¼ **cup chopped green onions**
¼ **cup red wine vinegar**
4 **teaspoons olive or vegetable oil**
½ **teaspoon dried basil leaves, crushed**

• Stir together pineapple and remaining ingredients in large bowl. Cover; chill 1 hour or overnight to blend flavors. Stir before serving.
                    Makes 10 servings

Prep Time: 20 minutes
Chill Time: 1 hour

Marinated Bean and Vegetable Salad

Bow Tie Pasta Salad

1 package (16 ounces) uncooked bow ties, rotini, ziti or other
shaped pasta
1 bag (16 ounces) BIRDS EYE® frozen Farm Fresh Mixtures
Broccoli, Cauliflower and Carrots*
1 cup Italian, creamy Italian or favorite salad dressing
1 bunch green onions, thinly sliced
1 cup pitted ripe olives, halved (optional)

Or, substitute any other Birds Eye® frozen Farm Fresh Mixtures variety.

• Cook pasta according to package directions; drain.

• Cook vegetables according to package directions; drain.

• Combine pasta and vegetables with remaining ingredients in large
bowl. Cover and chill until ready to serve.

Makes about 8 side-dish servings

Prep Time: 5 minutes
Cook Time: 20 minutes

Serving Suggestion: Use this recipe as the base for a variety of
main-dish salads, adding sliced salami and small cubes of cheese or
cooked chicken, turkey or seafood to the pasta and vegetables.

Bow Tie Pasta Salad

Twice Baked Potatoes

3 hot baked potatoes, split lengthwise
½ cup sour cream
2 tablespoons butter or margarine
1⅓ cups *French's*® French Fried Onions, divided
1 cup (4 ounces) shredded Cheddar cheese, divided
Dash paprika (optional)

1. Preheat oven to 400°F. Scoop out inside of potatoes into medium bowl, leaving thin shells. Mash potatoes with sour cream and butter until smooth. Stir in ⅔ *cup* French Fried Onions and ½ cup cheese. Spoon mixture into shells.

2. Bake 20 minutes or until heated through. Top with remaining cheese, onions and paprika, if desired. Bake 2 minutes or until cheese melts.

Makes 6 servings

Tip: To bake potatoes quickly, microwave on HIGH 10 to 12 minutes until tender.

Variation: For added Cheddar flavor, substitute *French's*® **Cheddar French Fried Onions** for the original flavor.

Twice Baked Potatoes

Vegetable Gratin

2 tablespoons olive oil
3 small *or* 1 large zucchini, cut into ¼-inch slices
⅛ teaspoon salt, divided
⅛ teaspoon dried thyme, divided
⅛ teaspoon dried rosemary, divided
⅛ teaspoon freshly ground black pepper, divided
1 (6.5-ounce) package ALOUETTE® Savory Vegetable
2 cups fresh broccoli florets
2 small yellow squash, sliced
1 small onion, sliced
1 cup crushed BRETON® Wheat Crackers

• Preheat oven to 350°F. Place oil in medium-sized gratin or shallow baking dish.

• Layer zucchini in prepared dish.

• Sprinkle zucchini lightly with half each of salt, thyme, rosemary and pepper.

• Place 3 tablespoons Alouette on top of zucchini.

• Layer with broccoli, yellow squash, onion, remaining seasonings and Alouette until dish is filled.

• Sprinkle with cracker crumbs; cover with foil. Bake 20 minutes.

• Remove foil; bake another 20 minutes. Brown lightly under broiler 1 to 2 minutes. Serve hot or at room temperature.   *Makes 6 to 8 servings*

Note: This gratin is a delicious way to liven up vegetables! It's great with grilled chicken or steak.

Vegetable Gratin

Spinach-Melon Salad

6 cups torn stemmed washed spinach
4 cups mixed melon balls, such as cantaloupe, honeydew and/or watermelon
1 cup sliced zucchini
½ cup sliced red bell pepper
¼ cup thinly sliced red onion
¼ cup red wine vinegar
2 tablespoons honey
2 teaspoons olive oil
2 teaspoons lime juice
1 teaspoon poppy seeds
1 teaspoon dried mint

1. Combine spinach, melon balls, zucchini, bell pepper and onion in large bowl.

2. For dressing, combine vinegar, honey, oil, lime juice, poppy seeds and mint in small jar with tight-fitting lid; shake well.

3. Pour dressing over salad; toss gently to coat. *Makes 6 servings*

Easy Greek Salad

6 romaine lettuce leaves, torn into 1½-inch pieces
1 medium cucumber, peeled and sliced
1 medium tomato, chopped
½ cup sliced red onion
⅓ cup crumbled feta cheese
2 tablespoons extra-virgin olive oil
2 tablespoons lemon juice
1 teaspoon dried oregano
½ teaspoon salt

1. Combine lettuce, cucumber, tomato, onion and cheese in large serving bowl.

2. Whisk together oil, lemon juice, oregano and salt in small bowl. Pour over lettuce mixture; toss until coated. Serve immediately.

Makes 6 servings

Prep Time: 10 minutes

Serving Suggestion: This simple but delicious salad makes a great accompaniment for grilled steaks or chicken.

Spinach-Melon Salad

Main Dishes

Super Hero Sandwich

- 1 (1-pound) loaf frozen bread dough, thawed
- ¾ cup mayonnaise or salad dressing
- 2 tablespoons Dijon mustard
- 2 teaspoons sugar
- 2 drops hot pepper sauce
- 1½ cups shredded Cheddar cheese
- 12 to 16 fresh spinach leaves
- 8 ounces thinly sliced CURE 81® ham
- 12 cucumber slices

Roll bread dough into a rope about 20 inches long; place on greased baking sheet. Form dough into ring; pinch ends together to seal. Place greased custard cup or empty metal can in center of ring. Cover dough. Let rise in warm place 1 hour or until doubled in size. Cut several diagonal slashes in top of dough with sharp knife, if desired. Heat oven to 375°F. Bake for 20 minutes or until golden brown.

In bowl, combine mayonnaise, mustard, sugar and hot pepper sauce; mix well. Stir in cheese. Slice bread ring in half horizontally. Spread each half with cheese mixture. Arrange spinach, ham and cucumber slices on bottom half of bread ring; cover with top. Secure with wooden picks. Cut into wedges to serve.

Makes 8 servings

Super Hero Sandwich

Tuscan Baked Rigatoni

1 pound Italian sausage, casings removed
1 pound rigatoni pasta, cooked, drained and kept warm
2 cups (8 ounces) shredded fontina cheese
2 tablespoons olive oil
2 fennel bulbs, thinly sliced
4 cloves garlic, minced
1 can (28 ounces) crushed tomatoes
1 cup heavy cream
1 teaspoon salt
1 teaspoon black pepper
8 cups coarsely chopped fresh spinach
1 can (15 ounces) cannellini beans, rinsed and drained
2 tablespoons pine nuts
½ cup grated Parmesan cheese

1. Preheat oven to 350°F. Spray 4-quart casserole with nonstick cooking spray. Crumble sausage in large skillet over medium-high heat. Cook and stir until no longer pink; drain. Transfer sausage to large bowl. Add pasta and fontina cheese; mix well.

2. Heat oil in same skillet; add fennel and garlic. Cook and stir over medium heat 3 minutes or until fennel is tender. Add tomatoes, cream, salt and pepper; cook and stir until slightly thickened. Stir in spinach, beans and pine nuts; cook until heated through.

3. Pour tomato sauce mixture over pasta and sausage; toss to coat. Transfer to prepared casserole; sprinkle evenly with Parmesan cheese. Bake 30 minutes or until hot and bubbly. *Makes 6 to 8 servings*

Tuscan Baked Rigatoni

Pork and Plum Kabobs

¾ **pound boneless pork loin chops (1 inch thick), trimmed of fat and cut into 1-inch pieces**
1½ **teaspoons ground cumin**
½ **teaspoon ground cinnamon**
¼ **teaspoon salt**
¼ **teaspoon garlic powder**
¼ **teaspoon ground red pepper**
¼ **cup no-sugar-added red raspberry spread**
¼ **cup sliced green onions**
1 **tablespoon orange juice**
3 **plums, pitted and cut into wedges**

1. Place pork in large resealable food storage bag. Combine cumin, cinnamon, salt, garlic powder and red pepper in small bowl. Sprinkle over meat in bag; seal bag. Shake to coat meat with spices.

2. Prepare grill for direct grilling. Combine raspberry spread, green onions and orange juice in small bowl; set aside.

3. Alternately thread pork and plum wedges onto 8 skewers.* Grill kabobs directly over medium heat 12 to 14 minutes or until meat is barely pink in center, turning once during grilling. Brush frequently with reserved raspberry mixture during last 5 minutes of grilling.

Makes 4 servings

If using wooden skewers, soak in water 20 minutes before using to prevent burning.

Serving Suggestion: A crisp, cool salad makes a great accompaniment to these sweet grilled kabobs.

Pork and Plum Kabobs

Curried Chicken Salad Sandwiches

1 (2- to 3-pound) whole roasted chicken*
1¼ cups halved seedless red grapes
½ cup diced Granny Smith apple
½ cup sliced almonds, toasted
⅓ cup golden raisins
⅓ cup dried cranberries
¼ cup unsweetened shredded coconut
¼ cup finely diced red onion
1 stalk celery, diced
¾ cup mayonnaise
1 tablespoon curry powder
1 tablespoon fresh lime juice
2 teaspoons honey
10 croissants
10 leaves red leaf lettuce
20 slices tomato

*You can substitute 3½ cups diced cooked chicken.

1. Remove skin and bones from chicken; dice meat. Combine chicken, grapes, apple, almonds, raisins, cranberries, coconut, onion and celery in large bowl; set aside.

2. Combine mayonnaise, curry powder, lime juice and honey in medium bowl. Add mayonnaise mixture to chicken mixture; stir until well blended. Season to taste with salt and black pepper.

3. Cut croissants in half horizontally. For each sandwich, line bottom half of 1 croissant with 1 leaf lettuce; top with about ¾ cup chicken salad and 2 slices tomato. Cover with top half of croissant.

Makes 10 sandwiches

Curried Chicken Salad Sandwich

Veggie No Boiling Lasagna

- **1 tablespoon olive oil**
- **1 medium sweet onion, thinly sliced**
- **1 medium red bell pepper, thinly sliced**
- **1 medium zucchini, cut in half lengthwise and thinly sliced**
- **2 containers (15 ounces each) ricotta cheese**
- **2 cups shredded mozzarella cheese (about 8 ounces), divided**
- **½ cup grated Parmesan cheese, divided**
- **2 eggs**
- **2 jars (1 pound 10 ounces each) RAGÚ® Old World Style® Pasta Sauce**
- **12 uncooked lasagna noodles**

Preheat oven to 375°F. In 12-inch nonstick skillet, heat olive oil over medium-high heat and cook onion, red bell pepper and zucchini, stirring occasionally, 5 minutes or until softened.

Meanwhile, combine ricotta cheese, 1 cup mozzarella cheese, ¼ cup Parmesan cheese and eggs.

In 13×9-inch baking dish, spread 1 cup Pasta Sauce. Layer 4 uncooked noodles, then 1 cup Sauce, half of the ricotta mixture and half of the vegetables; repeat. Top with remaining uncooked noodles and 2 cups Sauce. Reserve remaining Sauce.

Cover with foil and bake 1 hour. Remove foil; sprinkle with remaining cheeses. Bake uncovered 10 minutes. Let stand 10 minutes before serving. Serve with reserved Pasta Sauce, heated.

Makes 12 servings

Prep Time: 15 minutes
Cook Time: 1 hour, 15 minutes

Veggie No Boiling Lasagna

Caramelized Onion and Olive Pizza

2 tablespoons olive oil
1½ pounds onions, thinly sliced
2 teaspoons fresh rosemary *or* 1 teaspoon dried rosemary
¼ cup water
1 tablespoon balsamic vinegar
1 cup California ripe olives, sliced
1 (12-inch) prebaked thick pizza crust
2 cups (8 ounces) shredded mozzarella cheese

Heat oil in medium nonstick skillet until hot. Add onions and rosemary. Cook, stirring frequently, until onions begin to brown and browned bits begin to stick to bottom of skillet, about 15 minutes. Stir in ¼ cup water; scrape up any browned bits. Reduce heat to medium-low and continue to cook, stirring occasionally, until onions are golden and sweet tasting, 15 to 30 minutes longer; add more water, 1 tablespoon at a time, if pan appears dry. Remove pan from heat and stir in vinegar, scraping up any browned bits from pan. Gently stir in olives. Place crust on pizza pan or baking sheet. Spoon onion mixture into center of crust. Sprinkle with cheese. Bake in 450°F oven until cheese is melted and just beginning to brown, about 15 minutes. Cut into wedges and serve warm.

Makes 8 to 10 servings

Prep Time: 15 minutes
Cook Time: about 1 hour

Favorite recipe from *California Olive Industry*

Caramelized Onion and Olive Pizza

Muffuletta

1 (9¾-ounce) jar green olive salad, drained and chopped
¼ cup pitted black olives, chopped
1 large stalk celery, finely chopped
1½ teaspoons TABASCO® brand Pepper Sauce, divided
1 (8-inch) round loaf crusty French or sourdough bread
3 tablespoons olive oil
4 ounces sliced baked ham
4 ounces sliced provolone cheese
4 ounces sliced salami

Combine green olive salad, black olives, celery and 1 teaspoon TABASCO® Sauce in medium bowl. Cut bread crosswise in half; remove some of soft inside from each half. Combine oil and remaining ½ teaspoon TABASCO® Sauce in small bowl. Brush mixture on inside of bread. Fill bottom with olive mixture. Top with ham, cheese and salami. Top with remaining bread half. Cut loaf into quarters.

Makes 4 to 6 servings

Note: To heat Muffuletta, preheat oven to 350°F. Before cutting, place sandwich on rack in oven and heat 10 minutes or until cheese is melted.

Roasted Garlic Parmesan Penne Primavera

1 box (16 ounces) penne pasta
1 medium carrot, cut into very thin strips
1 cup snow peas
1 small red bell pepper, cut into very thin strips
1 jar (1 pound) RAGÚ® Cheesy! Roasted Garlic Parmesan Sauce
½ cup chicken broth
⅛ teaspoon ground black pepper
⅛ teaspoon ground nutmeg (optional)

Cook pasta according to package directions, adding vegetables during last 3 minutes of cooking; drain. Return to saucepan and stir in Sauce, broth, black pepper and nutmeg; heat through. Sprinkle, if desired, with grated Parmesan cheese.

Makes 8 servings

Tip: To reheat leftovers (as if there'll be any!), microwave in a covered dish on High (100% power) for about 1 minute. If not heated through, stir and continue cooking, checking at 15-second intervals.

Muffuletta

Broccoli-Filled Chicken Roulade

2 cups broccoli florets
1 tablespoon water
¼ cup fresh parsley
1 cup diced red bell pepper
4 ounces cream cheese, softened
2 tablespoons grated Parmesan cheese
2 tablespoons lemon juice
2 tablespoons olive oil
1 teaspoon paprika
¼ teaspoon salt
1 egg
½ cup fat-free (skim) milk
4 cups cornflakes, crushed
1 tablespoon dried basil
8 boneless skinless chicken breast halves

1. Place broccoli and water in microwavable dish; cover. Microwave on HIGH 2 minutes. Let stand, covered, 2 minutes. Drain water from broccoli. Place broccoli in food processor or blender. Add parsley; process 10 seconds, scraping side of bowl if necessary. Add bell pepper, cream cheese, Parmesan cheese, lemon juice, oil, paprika and salt. Pulse 2 to 3 times or until bell pepper is minced.

2. Preheat oven to 375°F. Spray 11×7-inch baking pan with nonstick cooking spray. Lightly beat egg in small bowl. Add milk; blend well. Place cornflake crumbs in shallow bowl. Add basil; blend well.

3. Pound chicken breasts between two pieces of plastic wrap to ¼-inch thickness using flat side of meat mallet or rolling pin. Spread each chicken breast with one eighth of broccoli mixture, spreading to within ½ inch of edges. Roll up chicken breast from short end, tucking in sides if possible; secure with toothpicks. Dip roulades in milk mixture; roll in cornflake crumb mixture. Place in prepared baking pan. Bake 20 minutes or until chicken is no longer pink in center and juices run clear. Garnish as desired. *Makes 8 servings*

Broccoli-Filled Chicken Roulade

Fettuccine Carbonara

1 box (12 ounces) fettuccine noodles
1 cup frozen green peas
1 jar (1 pound) RAGÚ® Cheesy! Light Parmesan Alfredo Sauce
4 slices turkey bacon, crisp-cooked and crumbled

Cook fettuccine according to package directions, adding peas during last 2 minutes of cooking; drain and set aside.

In 2-quart saucepan, heat Light Parmesan Alfredo Sauce over medium heat; stir in bacon.

To serve, toss sauce with hot fettuccine and peas. Sprinkle, if desired, with ground black pepper and grated Parmesan cheese.

Makes 6 servings

Prep Time: 5 minutes
Cook Time: 15 minutes

Pineapple Turkey Kabobs

1½ pounds boneless skinless turkey tenders
2 large red bell peppers
2 cups fresh pineapple chunks
½ cup rice wine vinegar
¼ cup pickled ginger
2 teaspoons chopped garlic
½ teaspoon black pepper
Nonstick cooking spray

1. Soak 6 wooden skewers in water 20 minutes. Preheat oven to 400°F.

2. Cut turkey and bell peppers into bite-size pieces. Place turkey, bell peppers, pineapple, vinegar, pickled ginger, garlic and black pepper in resealable food storage bag. Seal bag; turn several times to coat all ingredients. Refrigerate 20 minutes.

3. Spray 11×9-inch baking pan with nonstick cooking spray. Thread pieces of bell pepper, turkey, ginger and pineapple onto 6 skewers. Discard any remaining marinade. Place skewers in prepared pan; cover with foil. Bake 20 to 25 minutes or until turkey is cooked through. Serve with rice, if desired.

Makes 6 servings

Fettuccine Carbonara

Stromboli

¼ cup *French's®* Spicy Brown Mustard
2 tablespoons chopped fresh basil *or* 2 teaspoons dried basil
    leaves
1 tablespoon chopped green olives
1 pound frozen bread dough, thawed at room temperature
¼ pound sliced salami
¼ pound sliced provolone cheese
¼ pound sliced ham
⅛ pound thinly sliced pepperoni (2-inch diameter)
1 egg, beaten
1 teaspoon poppy or sesame seeds

1. Grease baking sheet. Stir mustard, basil and olives in small bowl; set aside.

2. Roll dough on floured surface to 16×10-inch rectangle.* Arrange salami on dough, overlapping slices, leaving 1-inch border around edges. Spread half of the mustard mixture thinly over salami. Arrange provolone and ham over salami. Spread with remaining mustard mixture. Top with pepperoni.

3. Fold one third of dough toward center from long edge of rectangle. Fold second side toward center enclosing filling. Pinch long edge to seal. Pinch short ends together and tuck under dough. Place on prepared baking sheet. Cover; let rise in warm place 15 minutes.

4. Preheat oven to 375°F. Cut shallow crosswise slits 3 inches apart on top of dough. Brush Stromboli lightly with beaten egg; sprinkle with poppy seeds. Bake 25 minutes or until browned. Remove to rack; cool slightly. Serve warm.   *Makes 12 servings*

If dough is too hard to roll, allow to rest on floured surface for 5 to 10 minutes.

Prep Time: 30 minutes
Cook Time: 25 minutes

Stromboli

Desserts & Treats

Cheesecake-Filled Strawberries

- 1 package (8 ounces) cream cheese, softened
- 1½ tablespoons powdered sugar
- 1½ teaspoons vanilla
- 1 pint strawberries
- 1 package (8 ounces) sliced almonds, toasted

1. Beat cream cheese 2 to 3 minutes in medium bowl with electric mixer at medium speed. Add powdered sugar and vanilla; beat until well blended.

2. Trim and discard stem ends from strawberries. Scoop out pulp, leaving ¼-inch shell; fill with cream cheese mixture. Top each strawberry with 2 toasted almonds.

3. Place strawberries on serving plate. Refrigerate until ready to serve.

Makes 4 to 6 servings

Variation: The strawberries can also be filled by cutting a wedge out of the side of each berry and scooping out the pulp, leaving about a ¼-inch shell. Fill the strawberries and arrange them as shown in the photo.

Cheesecake-Filled Strawberries

Monogrammed Mini Chocolate Cakes

½ **cup (1 stick) butter or margarine**
½ **cup water**
3 **tablespoons HERSHEY'S Cocoa**
1 **cup all-purpose flour**
1 **cup sugar**
½ **teaspoon baking soda**
¼ **teaspoon salt**
1 **egg**
⅓ **cup dairy sour cream**
  Cocoa Glaze (recipe follows)
  Decorating icing in tube, desired color

1. Heat oven to 350°F. Line bottom of 13×9×2-inch baking pan with parchment or wax paper.

2. Combine butter, ½ cup water and cocoa in small saucepan. Cook over medium heat, stirring constantly, until mixture boils; remove from heat. Stir together flour, sugar, baking soda and salt in medium bowl. Stir in hot cocoa mixture. Add egg and sour cream; beat on medium speed of mixer until well blended. Pour batter into prepared pan.

3. Bake 20 to 22 minutes or until wooden pick inserted in center comes out clean. Cool 10 minutes. Remove from pan to wire rack; carefully remove parchment paper. Cool completely.

4. Cut cake into small pieces, each about 2×1¾ inches. (Cake will be easier to cut if frozen for several hours or up to several days.) Place on wire cooling rack. Prepare Cocoa Glaze; spoon over top of each piece of cake, allowing glaze to run down sides. Allow glaze to set. Garnish with monogram, using decorating icing. Place in foil cup, if desired.

Makes about 24 mini cakes

Cocoa Glaze: Bring ½ cup water and ¼ cup (½ stick) butter to a boil in small saucepan. Stir in ½ cup HERSHEY'S Cocoa. Remove from heat; cool slightly. Gradually add 3 cups powdered sugar, stirring with whisk until smooth. Stir in 2 teaspoons vanilla extract. Makes about 1½ cups glaze.

Monogrammed Mini Chocolate Cakes

Passionate Profiteroles

Vanilla Custard Filling (recipe follows)
⅔ cup water
7 tablespoons plus 2 teaspoons I CAN'T BELIEVE IT'S NOT
    BUTTER!® Spread, divided
1 tablespoon sugar
¼ teaspoon salt
¾ cup all-purpose flour
4 large eggs
1 square (1 ounce) semi-sweet chocolate
Toasted sliced almonds (optional)

Prepare Vanilla Custard Filling. Preheat oven to 400°F. Lightly grease baking sheet; set aside. In 2½-quart saucepan, bring water, 7 tablespoons I Can't Believe It's Not Butter!® Spread, sugar and salt to a boil over high heat. Remove from heat and immediately stir in flour. Cook flour mixture over medium heat, stirring constantly with wooden spoon, 5 minutes or until film forms on bottom of pan. Remove from heat; stir in eggs, one at a time, beating well after each addition. Immediately drop by heaping tablespoonfuls onto prepared baking sheet. Place baking sheet on middle rack in oven. Bake 20 minutes.

Decrease oven temperature to 350°F; bake an additional 20 minutes. Turn off oven without opening door; let profiteroles stand in oven 10 minutes. Cool completely on wire rack. To fill, slice off top ⅓ of profiteroles; set aside. Fill with Vanilla Custard Filling. Replace tops.

In small microwave-safe bowl, microwave chocolate and remaining 2 teaspoons I Can't Believe It's Not Butter! Spread at HIGH (Full Power) 30 seconds or until melted; stir until smooth. Drizzle profiteroles with chocolate; sprinkle, if desired, with almonds.   *Makes 16 servings*

Vanilla Custard Filling

1 package (3.4 ounces) instant vanilla pudding mix
1 cup milk
3 to 4 tablespoons hazelnut, coffee, almond, orange or cherry
    liqueur (optional)
½ teaspoon vanilla extract
2 cups whipped cream or non-dairy whipped topping

In medium bowl, with wire whisk, blend pudding mix, milk, liqueur and vanilla. Fold in whipped cream. Cover with plastic wrap and refrigerate 1 hour or until set.

Passionate Profiteroles

Chocolate Truffle Cups

1 (7-ounce) package ALOUETTE® Cuisine™ Crème Fraîche
8 ounces good quality white or bittersweet chocolate, broken
    into small pieces
1 tablespoon liqueur, such as almond, coffee or orange
    (optional)
1 (2-ounce) package frozen mini phyllo shells

Heat crème fraîche over medium heat until it softens to a thick liquid
consistency. Remove from heat and add chocolate. Stir until chocolate is
melted and mixture is smooth. Add liqueur, if desired. Refrigerate for
1 hour or until set. Pipe into phyllo shells and serve.

Makes 15 dessert cups

Berry-Berry Brownie Torte

½ cup all-purpose flour
¼ teaspoon baking soda
¼ teaspoon salt
1 cup HERSHEY'S Semi-Sweet Chocolate Chips
½ cup (1 stick) butter or margarine
1¼ cups sugar, divided
2 eggs
1 teaspoon vanilla extract
⅓ cup HERSHEY'S SPECIAL DARK® Cocoa
½ cup whipping cream
¾ cup fresh blackberries, rinsed and patted dry
¾ cup fresh raspberries, rinsed and patted dry

1. Heat oven to 350°F. Line 9-inch round baking pan with wax paper,
then grease. Stir together flour, baking soda and salt. Stir in chocolate
chips.

2. Melt butter in medium saucepan over low heat. Remove from heat.
Stir in 1 cup sugar, eggs and vanilla. Add cocoa, blending well. Stir in
flour mixture. Spread mixture in prepared pan.

3. Bake 20 to 25 minutes or until wooden pick inserted into center
comes out slightly sticky. Cool in pan on wire rack 15 minutes. Invert
onto wire rack; remove wax paper. Turn right side up; cool completely.

4. Beat whipping cream and remaining ¼ cup sugar until sugar is
dissolved and stiff peaks form. Spread over top of brownie. Top with
berries. Refrigerate until serving time. *Makes 8 to 10 servings*

Chocolate Truffle Cups

Cracker Toffee

72 butter-flavored crackers
1 cup (2 sticks) unsalted butter
1 cup packed brown sugar
¼ teaspoon salt
2½ cups semisweet chocolate chips
2 cups chopped pecans

1. Preheat oven to 375°F. Line 17×12-inch jelly-roll pan with heavy-duty foil. Spray generously with nonstick cooking spray. Arrange crackers in pan; set aside.

2. Combine butter, sugar and salt in heavy medium saucepan. Heat over medium heat until butter melts, stirring frequently. Increase heat to high; boil 3 minutes without stirring. Pour mixture evenly over crackers; spread to cover.

3. Bake 5 minutes. Immediately sprinkle chocolate chips evenly over crackers; spread to cover. Sprinkle pecans over chocolate, pressing down. Cool to room temperature. Refrigerate 2 hours. Break into chunks to serve.   *Makes 24 servings*

Variation: Substitute peanut butter chips for chocolate chips and coarsely chopped, lightly salted peanuts for chopped pecans.

Cracker Toffee

Piña Colada Cake

Cake
   1 package (18¼ ounces) white cake mix, plus ingredients to
      prepare mix
Rum Filling
   ½ cup cold whipping cream
   ¼ cup dark rum
   2 tablespoons powdered sugar
   ¾ teaspoon vanilla
Whipped Topping
   2 cups cold whipping cream
   ¾ cup powdered sugar
   2 teaspoons vanilla
Garnishes
   1 fresh pineapple, peeled, cut in half lengthwise and cored
   2 cups sweetened shredded coconut, toasted*

To toast coconut, spread evenly on ungreased cookie sheet. Toast in preheated 350°F oven 5 to 7 minutes, stirring occasionally, until light golden brown.

1. Prepare cake mix and bake according to package directions using two 9-inch round cake pans. Cool in pans on wire racks 15 minutes. Remove cakes from pans; cool completely.

2. For rum filling, combine all ingredients in small bowl until well blended. Cover with plastic wrap; refrigerate until ready to use.

3. For whipped topping, place 2 cups whipping cream in large bowl; beat 1½ to 2 minutes or until soft peaks form. Add powdered sugar and vanilla; beat 20 seconds or until stiff peaks form. Cover with plastic wrap; refrigerate until ready to use.

4. Place pineapple cut side down on cutting board; slice very thinly. Place slices on paper towels; pat dry.

5. Place 1 cake layer on serving plate. Spread half of rum filling evenly over cake. Spread 1 cup whipped topping evenly over cake. Sprinkle with 1 cup coconut; top with remaining cake layer. Spread remaining rum filling evenly over cake. Spread remaining whipped topping evenly over top and side of cake; sprinkle top with remaining coconut.

6. Press pineapple slices around side of cake vertically, overlapping slightly. Reserve any remaining pineapple slices for another use. Refrigerate cake until ready to serve. *Makes 12 servings*

Piña Colada Cake

Quick Berry Trifle

        2 cups sliced strawberries
        1 cup fresh raspberries or blackberries
        1 cup fresh blueberries
        ¼ cup sugar
        1 pound cake (about 12 ounces), cut into ½-inch-thick slices
        1 container (28 ounces) prepared vanilla pudding
        1 can (7 ounces) aerosol whipped topping

1. Place berries and sugar in medium bowl; stir gently to blend.

2. Place single layer of cake slices in bottom of deep serving bowl. Top with one third of pudding and one third of berries. Repeat layers twice, ending with berries. Cover tightly with plastic wrap; refrigerate at least 1 hour or until ready to serve.

3. Just before serving, garnish with whipped topping.

Makes 12 servings

Dessert Grape Clusters

        2 pounds seedless red and/or green grapes
        1 pound premium white chocolate, coarsely chopped
        2 cups finely chopped honey-roasted cashews

1. Rinse grapes under cold running water in colander; drain well. Cut grapes into clusters of 3 grapes with kitchen shears. Place clusters in single layer on paper towels. Let stand at room temperature until completely dry.

2. Melt white chocolate in top of double boiler over hot, not boiling, water. Stir until white chocolate is melted. Remove from heat.

3. Place cashews in shallow bowl. Working with 1 cluster at a time, holding by stem, dip grapes into melted chocolate; allow excess to drain back into pan. Roll grapes gently in cashews. Place grapes, stem sides up, on waxed paper; repeat with remaining clusters. Refrigerate until firm. Serve within 4 hours.

Makes about 3 dozen clusters (2½ pounds)

Quick Berry Trifle

Nancy's Tiramisu

        6 **egg yolks**
    1¼ **cups sugar**
    1½ **cups mascarpone cheese**
    1¾ **cups whipping cream, beaten to soft peaks**
    1¾ **cups cold espresso or strong brewed coffee**
        3 **tablespoons brandy**
        3 **tablespoons grappa**
      48 **ladyfingers**
        2 **tablespoons unsweetened cocoa powder, divided**

1. Beat egg yolks and sugar in small bowl with electric mixer on medium-high speed until pale yellow. Place in top of double boiler over boiling water. Reduce heat to low; cook, stirring constantly, 10 minutes. Combine yolk mixture and mascarpone cheese in large bowl; beat with electric mixer at low speed until well blended and fluffy. Fold in whipped cream. Set aside.

2. Combine espresso, brandy and grappa in medium bowl. Dip 24 ladyfingers, one at a time, in espresso mixture and arrange in single layer in 13×9-inch glass baking dish. (Dip ladyfingers into mixture quickly or they will absorb too much liquid and fall apart.)

3. Spread half of mascarpone mixture over ladyfingers. Sift 1 tablespoon cocoa over mascarpone layer. Dip remaining 24 ladyfingers in espresso mixture and repeat layers.

4. Refrigerate overnight or at least 4 hours. Cut into squares to serve.

Makes 12 servings

Substitution: If mascarpone cheese is unavailable, combine 1 package (8 ounces) softened cream cheese, ¼ cup sour cream and 2 tablespoons whipping cream in medium bowl. Beat 2 minutes with electric mixer at medium speed until light and fluffy.

Nancy's Tiramisu

Nutty Toffee Ice Cream Cake

1 package (18¼ ounces) devil's food cake mix, plus ingredients
   to prepare mix
2 quarts vanilla ice cream, slightly softened
1½ cups toffee baking bits, divided
1 container (14 ounces) cream-filled pirouette cookies (about
   30 cookies)
1 container (16 ounces) chocolate frosting
¾ cup unsalted peanuts or nut topping, toasted and chopped
   Ribbon (optional)

1. Prepare cake mix and bake according to package directions using
two 9-inch round cake pans. Cool in pans on wire racks 15 minutes.
Remove from pans; cool completely on wire racks.

2. Place 1 cake layer on serving plate. Spread 4 cups softened ice cream
evenly over cake. Sprinkle with ¾ cup toffee bits. Top with remaining
cake layer. Spread remaining 4 cups ice cream evenly over top of cake.
Wrap with plastic wrap coated with nonstick cooking spray; freeze
about 30 minutes.

3. Meanwhile, carefully cut each cookie in half lengthwise with sharp
serrated knife.

4. Remove cake from freezer. Frost side only with chocolate frosting.
Place cookie halves vertically around side of cake. Sprinkle nuts and
remaining ¾ cup toffee bits over top of cake. Wrap with plastic wrap;
freeze overnight or at least 8 hours until very firm. Tie ribbon around
cake before serving, if desired.   *Makes 12 servings*

Variation: For a beautiful holiday look, substitute candy canes for
the pirouette cookies and crushed peppermint candies for the nuts and
toffee bits.

Nutty Toffee Ice Cream Cake

Strawberry Daiquiri Dessert

1 package (3 ounces) ladyfingers, thawed if frozen, split in half horizontally
2 tablespoons light rum or apricot nectar
1 container (8 ounces) thawed frozen nondairy whipped topping, divided
1 package (8 ounces) cream cheese, softened
1 package (16 ounces) frozen strawberries, thawed
1 can (10 ounces) frozen strawberry daiquiri mix, thawed
Fresh strawberries (optional)

1. Place ladyfinger halves, cut side up, in bottom of 11×7-inch dish. Brush with rum.

2. Place 1 cup whipped topping in small bowl; cover with plastic wrap and refrigerate until ready to use.

3. Place cream cheese in food processor; process until fluffy. Add remaining whipped topping, thawed frozen strawberries and daiquiri mix; process with on/off pulses until blended. Pour over ladyfingers.

4. Freeze 6 hours or overnight. Remove from freezer. Allow dish to stand at room temperature 20 to 30 minutes before serving. Garnish with remaining whipped topping and fresh strawberries, if desired. Store leftovers in freezer.   *Makes 10 servings*

Acknowledgments

The publisher would like to thank the companies and organizations listed below for the use of their recipes and photographs in this publication.

Alouette® Cheese, Chavrie® Cheese, Saladena®, Montrachet®

Birds Eye Foods

Bob Evans®

California Olive Industry

Cherry Marketing Institute

Del Monte Corporation

Dole Food Company, Inc.

Florida Department of Agriculture and Consumer Services, Bureau of Seafood and Aquaculture

Guiltless Gourmet®

The Hershey Company

The Hidden Valley® Food Products Company

Hillshire Farm®

Holland House® is a registered trademark of Mott's, LLP

Hormel Foods, LLC

McIlhenny Company (TABASCO® brand Pepper Sauce)

National Chicken Council / US Poultry & Egg Association

North Dakota Beef Commission

Ortega®, A Division of B&G Foods, Inc.

Peanut Advisory Board

Reckitt Benckiser Inc.

Sargento® Foods Inc.

Sonoma® Dried Tomatoes

Unilever

Index

METRIC CONVERSION CHART

VOLUME MEASUREMENTS (dry)

1/8 teaspoon = 0.5 mL
1/4 teaspoon = 1 mL
1/2 teaspoon = 2 mL
3/4 teaspoon = 4 mL
1 teaspoon = 5 mL
1 tablespoon = 15 mL
2 tablespoons = 30 mL
1/4 cup = 60 mL
1/3 cup = 75 mL
1/2 cup = 125 mL
2/3 cup = 150 mL
3/4 cup = 175 mL
1 cup = 250 mL
2 cups = 1 pint = 500 mL
3 cups = 750 mL
4 cups = 1 quart = 1 L

VOLUME MEASUREMENTS (fluid)

1 fluid ounce (2 tablespoons) = 30 mL
4 fluid ounces (1/2 cup) = 125 mL
8 fluid ounces (1 cup) = 250 mL
12 fluid ounces (1 1/2 cups) = 375 mL
16 fluid ounces (2 cups) = 500 mL

WEIGHTS (mass)

1/2 ounce = 15 g
1 ounce = 30 g
3 ounces = 90 g
4 ounces = 120 g
8 ounces = 225 g
10 ounces = 285 g
12 ounces = 360 g
16 ounces = 1 pound = 450 g

DIMENSIONS

1/16 inch = 2 mm
1/8 inch = 3 mm
1/4 inch = 6 mm
1/2 inch = 1.5 cm
3/4 inch = 2 cm
1 inch = 2.5 cm

OVEN TEMPERATURES

250°F = 120°C
275°F = 140°C
300°F = 150°C
325°F = 160°C
350°F = 180°C
375°F = 190°C
400°F = 200°C
425°F = 220°C
450°F = 230°C

BAKING PAN SIZES

Utensil	Size in Inches/Quarts	Metric Volume	Size in Centimeters
Baking or Cake Pan (square or rectangular)	8×8×2	2 L	20×20×5
	9×9×2	2.5 L	23×23×5
	12×8×2	3 L	30×20×5
	13×9×2	3.5 L	33×23×5
Loaf Pan	8×4×3	1.5 L	20×10×7
	9×5×3	2 L	23×13×7
Round Layer Cake Pan	8×1½	1.2 L	20×4
	9×1½	1.5 L	23×4
Pie Plate	8×1¼	750 mL	20×3
	9×1¼	1 L	23×3
Baking Dish or Casserole	1 quart	1 L	—
	1½ quart	1.5 L	—
	2 quart	2 L	—